Treasure in Earthen Vessels

ISBN: 1-894696-34-4

Writers/Editors: Dr. James Humphries/Betty Giesbrecht
Printed in Canada by
Project L.A.M.B.S. International Inc.
Box 20569
Steinbach, Manitoba
R5G 1R9

Phone 1-204-346-5708
E-mail: projectlambs@mts.net
website: www.projectlambs.com

1st Edition, August 2005

Library and Archives Canada Cataloguing in Publication

Humphries, James P. (James Paul), 1954-
Treasure in Earthen Vessels : A Tribute to the Life of Reverend Irene Humphries 1950-2005 / by James P. Humphries ; Betty Giesbrecht, editor.

ISBN 1-894696-34-4

1. Humphries, Irene, 1950-2005. 2. Project L.A.M.B.S. 3. Bible colleges. I. Giesbrecht, Betty II. Project L.A.M.B.S. III. Title.

BV1470.3.H85H85 2005 230'.071'1 C2005-905221-X

CONTENTS

Dedication

This booklet is dedicated to all those brothers and sisters worldwide that carried and walked with Irene in the last years of her journey here on earth. The body of Christ has been our fortress and strength and the Holy Spirit was truly, our comforter and guide. Your love, prayers and support had an everlasting effect for all eternity on our sister and friend. The body of Jesus Christ truly rose to the occasion and met all the needs of servant Irene. Some day, Lord willing Irene will thank you personally.

The Bible also shares that we should give honour where honour is due, and through this little publication, we wish to honour first and foremost our King Jesus Christ, and secondly the life of Irene, who Christ walked and flowed through.

Peter 3:7
Husbands, likewise, dwell with them with understanding,
Give honour to the wife, as to the weaker vessel,
And as being heirs together of the grace of life,
that your prayers will not be hindered.

As a husband to Irene, I have chosen to honour her with a small tribute book that I pray God will use to minister to those who may read it.

Introduction

This little booklet was birthed out of the challenges of walking with Irene Humphries during her last days where she battled intently with cancer. Irene went home to be with the Lord Jesus Christ on March 9, 2005, eleven days before her 55th birthday and eighteen hours after her 5th grandchild was born; Anna-Irene Prairie Humphries.

What follows is, I believe, God's way of helping me by His Holy Spirit to get a proper God-given perspective on all that happened to Irene and me, my family and friends. This last part of Irene's pilgrimage lasted about two and half years and the road was full of many twists, turns, valleys and mountain tops. I saw Irene being transformed, as it were; a metamorphism, a breaking out of this earthly shell into a radiant daughter of Christ; a cup-bearer of the Most High, one who was sweet smelling incense to all who came in contact with her.

This message was given to me one day just after the funeral. The phrase " we have a treasure in an earthen vessel" kept going through my mind over and over again, and I could not get released of it until I began to study in the Bible and to allow the Holy Spirit to speak into my life, the truth of what it all meant and what it would mean to me as one who has just helped his best friend walk the shadows of death.

I do mourn deeply, not as one who has no hope, but as one who through Jesus Christ has been given much grace and peace from my King. The coals have not gone out; they are

being stoked so that once again out of these ashes will come a fire that burns for His glory.

I see now that God was putting his finishing touches on the treasure. The vessel underwent much pain and suffering but the treasure came through as priceless, prepared and handled only as the Master with all His wisdom and understanding could. God has truly kept and fulfilled all His promises and covenants to Irene.

I pray that this little booklet will minister to you and bring honour and glory to our Lord Jesus Christ. It was freely given to me, and now I share with you this tribute to Irene's life.

Your servant in Christ,

Jim

II Corinthians 1:4

CHAPTER ONE

Treasure in Earthen Vessels

INTRODUCTION:

The way one looks at things each day will determine how one will react and respond to the day's events. I knew that my day and my life were soon to go through a major change. My wife Irene was in a palliative care unit in St. Boniface hospital in Winnipeg, battling with severe pain from ovarian cancer that had spread to various parts of her body. The doctors had told me that we were now down to maybe a few days or just hours.

March 8th had arrived and my son Joshua and Donna his wife were about to give to us our fifth grandchild. By 6:15 little Anna–Irene Prairie entered the world over at the Health Science Centre in Winnipeg, I went to see them. Not long afterwards, our friend Matilda Fehr called me on the cell phone; she told me that Irene was going through another severe pain crisis.

I returned to St. Boniface with a video of our new grand child. Even though Irene was very weak, Matilda and I open up her eyelids so that she could see our new gift from God. Irene began to weep and Matilda and I encouraged her to go home to be with Christ. Everything was fine; God had blessed us again.

The night was long and we kept praying that God would show His mercy and release Irene from this body of pain. The morning came and Irene was resting. I quickly went over to see our new grandchild again. What a special gift from God.

After I came back Irene's breathing seemed to have worsened, but the head doctor felt that it could still be another few days yet. I went again to Irene and told her that everything was fine with Josh, Donna and Prairie and that she should now go home to be with the Lord. To the doctors' and nurses' surprise, with me holding her hand, Irene took these last few steps into the everlasting Kingdom of Christ at 12:12 noon. The moment I had both prayed for and dreaded was now fixed in time for all history.

Irene had crossed over into eternity. She was now at peace and the process of breaking away from the pain and suffering of this life was finally over. She could not wait to see Jesus and now she was in His very presence. All the dreams that she had had of heaven were now reality for her. The list of all the names that she had written in her diary, people that she was looking forward to seeing were now all welcoming her home. The metamorphosis was complete; she was now flying like an eagle above all the storms and challenges of this life.

A few days later, after the funeral and when all the family and friends had gone home, my mind got to thinking more deeply about things concerning the Word of God, and the one thing that would not leave my mind was a phrase of Scripture from II Corinthians 4, "treasure in earthen vessels".

As a discipleship trainer that has been blessed together with Irene to travel to many different parts of the world, I know that God's word is full of many discipleship keys that can help us through any challenges and struggles that we face. I do not grieve as one who has no hope, but I do grieve as one who has lost a mentor, teacher and close friend and companion for almost thirty-three years.

If there is a regret that I have, now that Irene has gone home, it is that I sometimes did not realize or give thanks for the treasure in the earthen vessel that had been given to me by God. With Christ we have and are an awesome treasure. Christ saw the value and was willing to pay the price for it. He sees that value, significance and self worth in all of us, but we often do not see it in each other. How great a treasure that lay within Irene's vessel, not because she was my wife, but because she was God's child!

At the funeral and in all the letters and emails, phone calls and visits I received, I heard over and over again the testimony of this special treasure that God had given to the church for a season. I wish I had taken more time to give thanks to God. We did not know, even though she was amongst us, after what God had been doing and saying to us through her life. But there are so many others like that all around us, people who are gifts and treasures from God. Each one of us is like that, seeing and hearing but not really seeing and hearing at all. Irene's life showed how much out of alignment we are to what God is doing in our lives. He was and is doing great things in other people's lives all around us. I was too busy, too active in doing, overwhelmed by schedules, with so little time to see that there are God-given treasures all around me.

I see now that in North America we value things that are valueless but put no value on things that are of great value. Or to put it another way we value the package more than the content inside the package.

I just want to share with you, a few little insights that have come to me that I believe God wants us to see afresh from His word and from the life of Irene Humphries.

II Corinthians 4:6-12

"For God, who said, light shall shine out of darkness, is the One who has shone in our hearts to give the light of knowledge of the glory of God in the face of Christ. But we have this treasure in earthen vessels, so that the surpassing greatness of the power will be of God and not from ourselves; we are afflicted in every way, but not crushed; perplexed, but not despairing; persecuted, but not forsaken; struck down but not destroyed; always carrying about in the body the dying of Jesus, so that the life of Jesus also may be manifested in our body. For we who live are constantly being delivered over to death for Jesus' sake, so that the life of Jesus also may be manifested in our mortal flesh. So death works in us, but life in you."

I can say that over the last several months I saw Irene's life fulfilling this passage of Scripture to all its fullness. I saw great affliction, the crushing of cancer, the perplexity of it all, but God did not leave the room. His presence and strength were there all the time. His anointing was there. The grace of God was there. His perfect will was being accomplished.

From this book I want us to see that it is not the vessel that we are to be focusing on, but the treasure in the vessel. Yes, we have lost a great vessel, her name was Irene Humphries, but we have not lost a great treasure. The moment she stepped into eternity was the moment that God called that special treasure that He had created and moulded, home unto Himself.

I believe that God was trying to show me the bigger picture about our lives here on earth and our place of value to God in heaven. Over the next few pages I want to point out from Scripture, and also illustrate from Irene's life, four key words, that if understood correctly can be a foundation stone for revival in one's heart and in the local church. We as disciples must begin to see things, the way God sees them. We must view them from His point of view, not ours. We must see them according to his will and not our will.

There were four words that began to formulate in my mind not only from what Irene and I had gone through, but as an important discipleship principle that we all need to be aware of and keep focused on as we travel along our journey for Christ.

I would like draw to our attention four key points that will help us see the bigger picture of what it means to be a true disciple of Christ. These will help the disciple to see and understand the extreme importance of what God has placed inside each believer as a vessel, a treasure that is beyond value here on earth.

Each word is an object lesson that will unlock for us a door of truth. Please walk with me on this journey of exploration and I pray this testimony will touch your heart as it has moved mine.

The Vessel

≈≈≈≈≈≈≈≈≈

A vessel is just the container that holds and carries the content that you want to ship or move around. They come in all different sizes and shapes. The packaging may be colourful, attractive, and compelling to the eyes but it is still just a package that we will either discard or burn when we get home.

The dictionary defines **vessel** as; boat, craft, ship, container, pot, receptacle, and utensil. It is something that holds and protects something else of greater value.

The Bible tells us that we are all like "jars of clay" in all different shapes and sizes, formed from the clay of the earth and made by a master potter who lovingly forms us and makes us; then fired in a kiln to give us strength and shape. We are all uniquely different in a variety of ways. We have been created in such a way that we carry within us a substance of value, which is living and active.

As humans, and especially in North America, we are more concerned with the outward package than we are with the content inside. Eighty percent of what is in the garbage cans is just packages. Every week the garbage truck hauls all those packages to the dump. We do not take those packages and hang them on the wall or display them in some prominent place, but just discard them. The package is of little value.

Paul said, the package is going to decay, and be discarded and that out of that death a new creation is going to be made. Out of the ashes an ever-lasting vessel will come. This package here on earth is going to let you down. Verse four states that it will undergo affliction, perplexities, persecution and be struck down to the place where you feel like you are constantly dying.

But again we are not to treasure the package, but the treasure inside the package; Jesus is going to give us a new package. The contents were of such great value that Christ gave His life as a ransom to redeem the contents back from total destruction.

As a disciple we need to evaluate what it is that we are focused on here on earth. What do we hold on to so dearly? We need to get our eyes off the package and back on the treasure that Christ died for. The container will undergo much stress, strain and challenges and may even break down and die, but that is not the end of the journey for the contents inside.

I did not put the treasure of Irene in the gravesite; I just put the package there. The treasure was picked up by God's loving hands and escorted into heaven. I respect that package; it had value and it was important for a time. I will still go to the gravesite, because it is an earthly connection for me on how to handle what has happened in my own package. But what I will have to remember and focus on is the treasure that God gave to others and to me for those fifty-five years of Irene being here.

Pastor Broesky would tell Irene, "You are living in a glasshouse. Irene, you are a vessel that everyone is watching," he would say. The last part of her journey was a call to suffering for Christ's sake; a book that people would watch and read. Would she curse God or worship Him with all that she had? She was like Job who was watched by all his family and friends.

My wife and I didn't want that old container back or just to have it patched up. Her container in the last days was unable to hold, carry or contain the contents any more. It was evident that God was not going to raise up the container again, as He did in the past, so Irene would be able to continue on in that vessel for ministry. It was time for the old container to be discarded and a new heavenly one put in place.

My ministry, with Irene, my ministry was to help her to break out of the container and put her into the hands of Jesus who was going to give her a new body. The spirit of Irene was intact, but that container that housed her was undergoing decay. The time had come through prayers for the disciples to walk Irene through the shadow lands into the glorious kingdom of light where there would be no more darkness.

This is what Paul was trying to teach to the Corinthian Church, "For the God, who said, '*Light shall shine out of darkness*,' is the One who has shone in our hearts to give the Light of the knowledge of the glory of God in the face of Christ." (Verse 6)

People were discouraged about what was going on with Irene's vessel, but many also were encouraged about what was going on with the treasure. The treasure never changed, just the vessel did. When God called her home, the vessel would be discarded but the treasure was going to be glorifying God for all eternity.

The challenges that we face as a disciple are whether we are going to be a vessel for the world or vessels of honour for Christ. What are we filling up our containers with?

The "vessels of the world" are people that are putting all the focus on things and thinking of this world. They are building an earthly kingdom and not a heavenly one. When a person dies, all the effort and wealth is passed on to others either by selling, giving it away or just simply throwing it out. All that was stored up was just more container of wealth so that you could have gone out and bought more containers if you had time or desired to.

The world loves the container; even as believers we value the container way too much. The world is constantly enticing our flesh by the way it packages and displays the container. We are so often held hostage from serving the Lord Jesus Christ because of the power of the container.

As a disciple of Christ we are to be vessels for honour. Our outward vessel should and will reflect what is going on inside. When people see us they do see the outward person or the container. But our lives should be transparent enough so the world can see what is being carried about on the inside.

Each of us is a "cup bearer" of precious water so that you can go and give a drink to a thirsty soul. The vessel is used to carry the life-giving water, but it does not within itself have life-giving potential.

You are to be a jar of clay full of oil that will bring anointing and healing to the broken hearted. The disciple is to be a vessel of refreshing grace and hope to the weary traveller. The Holy Spirit is poured into us so we can be poured into others. Freely we have received, now freely we give out to others.

Christians need to focus on the contents of the container and value it. The ministry that Christ has gifted us with does not come from the container but from the anointing and power that flows through the treasure.

Matthew 7:20 says, "So then, you will know them by their fruit". Not by the container that holds the fruit but by the fruit itself. The container should and does most often advertise to the world what the contents that are found inside.

Religion focuses so much on the vessel or container but Christ focuses was on the content. The early apostles and disciples struggled so much with this very topic. Some took the position of righteousness coming through keeping certain laws, and the other camp was saying that righteousness came through faith in and the grace of Christ.

Galatians 6:15 says, *"for neither is circumcision anything, nor uncircumcision, but a new creation"*.

It is not what you do to the container that counts but it is what you do with the attitude and the treasure that is in our hearts. Will it be my will or Christ's will that needs to be fulfilled here on earth as it has been decreed in heaven?

In II Corinthians 5:17, Paul says *"Therefore if anyone is in Christ, he is a new creature; the old things passed away; behold, new things have come."*

The old will be transformed into the new if we will surrender our will to Christ's will. The vessel needs to be carrying the oil of the Holy Spirit. The Holy Spirit is what empowers the disciple to change, grow and mature in Christ to such a place that we will produce fruit that will last.

The Treasure

God has placed within man a treasure that is made up of a variety of parts and functions. They are like seeds, each having a key time for when they will germinate and come alive for His purpose.

The vessel is only the package and container that houses the true treasure. This is what Christ came to set us free from. He wants to release in us and through us to a lost world a treasure that cannot compare to anything that the world can offer.

The dictionary gives us some synonyms that can help better understand the word treasure. They are, " cash, fortune, funds, gold, riches, valuables, wealth, apple of one's eye, darling, gem, precious, pride and joy, prize, adore, cherish, esteem, hold dear, love, value, lay up, store up".

The treasure that God desires to work out through us has many aspects or pieces to it, and it is key that we see this unique treasure in all it fullness.

Talents – God has given you a mixture of talents that are unique only to you so that with them you can help, minister and bless others. It has been entrusted to you. It comes to you as a gift but you must in turn hone it into a tool that will be useful and a blessing to others that are around you. One of the many talents that Irene had, was that of being an artist; drawing and designing things. She was also an excellent communicator.

Attitude – The way we think affects everything we say and do each day. Our attitude will either bind us or free us. The mind is a gift that God gave to men and women that is unique and special over all creation.

The mind is the seed ground of your will. It is the place where you will battle between your will and God's will for your life.

Guard your attitude. I would always tell Irene, your thinking has to come into subjection to your spirit, not your spirit to your mind. Irene and I could either come through these trials and struggles and be very angry or come through it praising God, saying "my redeemer liveth". This journey that we were on made us feel like we were being crushed; it was very perplexing. While Irene was dying I died a thousand deaths as well.

The scripture tells us that, our bodies are afflicted, crushed and perplexed. The mind was our biggest battlefield and we needed each other to help keep focused. We are to have the mind of Christ.

Over and over I would have to remind Irene and myself that our bodies and minds must come into subjection and under the authority of the Spirit. God has given the spirit life and authority, but we must loosen and free Him daily in our lives. It is the spiritual man that has been given eternal life through Christ.

Fruit of the Spirit –We also have with us the fruit of the Spirit. When we receive Christ as Lord and Saviour we become a disciple of Christ. He pours within us life, like sap to a tree branch; and as that life flows through us it will produce out of us branches of fruit that others should be able to pick and enjoy. Your treasure, if released out to others, will produce and affect people's lives for all eternity.

People need to pick from our tree the life that is being treasured deep within our hearts by God. The fruit that should be produced from this treasure inside is love, joy, peace, gentleness, long suffering, kindness, meekness, goodness, faithfulness and self-control. (Galatians 5:22)

Irene was a strong testimony each day of God's fruit flowing forth to others. In fact, the name Irene means "peace".

Spiritual Gifts – God gave these to you so that you can minister to the church and help in breaking the world free from the grip of death. These gifts are the by-product that should come forth from the life that is filled with the fruit of the Spirit.

Break the world free of death. We are a vessel that carries around living waters. I carry life; I am not going to carry around my wife's death inside me. I will carry around her life and I will travel around the world telling people about life, not death. We can set the captive free. So much bondage and death is all around us. Christians seem to be mourning more than I am.

The gifts are God-given tools that God gives to the Body or the church of Christ to minister and care for each other.

Communication- Something else that is unique to man is all the different ways that we can express ourselves and communicate to one another. This is also another special aspect that God has created us with, so we can serve and minister to each other. God gifted Irene as a teacher and missionary.

She was able to communicate verbally and non-verbally. Often her very presence in a room would bring peace to those who were around her. Her smile and warmth caused people to want to know her and to be with her. People would come into her classrooms and be ushered immediately into a beautiful presence of God's love and peace. Everywhere we traveled people would want to just gather around her. She was not often a spellbinding communicator verbally, but non-verbally she could bring you into the presence of God just by a smile or a touch of her hand.

Time – This was also created by God for man to be used wisely. Time is the sting of death. We are fighting with time in all that we do and say. The older we get the faster it slips through our fingers. We need to be good stewards of time. I must use it wisely. The one regret I have is that I did not use my time wisely with my wife and my children and with my King Jesus. People say today that they have so little time. They thank God for how much time I gave to Irene. I valued that time. God in His love gave as a treasure the gift of time to me to fulfill a vow that I had made to Irene on our wedding day; "through sickness and in health."

Stewardship- When we become Disciples of Christ everything becomes His and then He entrusts it back to us as stewards to use it wisely for His glory. We need much wisdom and understanding in this area. Stewardship is not based on what we can receive but how we use that which we have been entrusted with. God had entrusted Irene into my hands as a gift from Him. We are to be investing in heaven not in things here on earth. We need to use each aspect of this treasure to help and to minister to each other.

Each one of these are given in rough form and the disciple is given time by God's grace and His help to mould them from a rough stone into a diamond that will glorify His name.

Christ showed to us that what we are, and who we are, was worth dying for. The challenge we face as believers is to train our mind and heart to look past the vessel and see God's special treasure in each person. God has created each man and woman and He died for them because of the value of the treasure that lies within each one.

The Scriptures again have some very key truths to point out to the disciple about this treasure that is within our earthly vessel.

Isaiah 33:6 "And He will be the stability of your times, a wealth of salvation, wisdom and knowledge; the fear of the Lord is his treasure".

Matthew 6:21 "For where your treasure is, there your heart will be also."

Matthew 13:44 " The kingdom of heaven is like a treasure hidden in the field, which a man found and hid again; and from joy over it he goes and sells all that he has and buys that field."

How great a treasure it is that God has placed in each one of us. Its value is priceless. Its power can move and change peoples hearts, and it lives for all eternity.

The Pouring Out

That treasure only has great value when it is poured out or invested in others. Look at the definition of the word pour: *let flow, spill, splash, emit, gush, run, rush, spew, spout, stream, rain.* These words give the idea of movement and action; we are not to be dormant or sitting still.

The woman who did the anointing of Jesus in the Bible is a good example to the disciples of how our actions can affect and touch other people's lives.

> Matthew 26:6-13 " *Now when Jesus was in Bethany, at the home of Simon the leper, a woman came to Him with an alabaster vial of very costly perfume, and she poured it on His head as He reclined at the table. But the disciples were indignant when they saw this, and said, why this waste? For the perfume might have been sold for a high price and the money given to the poor. But Jesus, aware of this, said to them, why do you bother the woman? For she has done a good deed to me. For you always have the poor with you, but you do not always have me. For when she poured this perfume on My body, she did it to prepare Me for burial. Truly I say to you, wherever this gospel is preached in the world, what this woman has done will also be spoken of in memory of her."*

The disciples said that they could have used that treasure differently; they could have helped the poor. They could only see the outward picture of what took place, but Jesus saw the heart of the woman and how her actions of pouring out an earthly treasure were putting up for her an eternal reward. Not only that but for thousand of years since, her gift of love is still being spoken of as part of the Gospel of Christ.

Many people came to me and said that with all that was going on in Irene's life it was a sad use of that treasure. They said she was so young and there is so much more she could do yet. But we did not know Irene on the inside. She was always willing to be broken open like a perfume bottle to anoint her King in love and to be a sweet smelling incense for the Lord unto the church and to a lost world. Her life was poured all over her Saviour Jesus Christ. It was not a waste at all. Her investment in all that she had will lay up great treasures in heaven, not for herself so much, but as a gift for her friend and King, Jesus Christ. The price was costly from a human point of view, but for her Lord it was worth it all.

She did not leave ahead of time but she was taken home by Christ at His divine calling. The joy was that she completed her race far sooner than most disciples. That which she was created for was now completed.

Even after her physical body is gone the fragrance continues to linger for God's glory. Nothing is lost or wasted. Most of all Irene's work and ministry were completed at the proper place and time. Her life of pain and suffering was never used for an excuse not to go and to serve. She would just cry out more in prayer and ask her heavenly Father to give the needed strength to make it through the next part of the journey. She experienced that a lot. The truth is that as she poured out physically, emotionally and spiritually, God poured in more of His love and strength so she could keep on keeping on. She wanted to be a cupbearer of God's oil; to be poured out to whomever according to His will.

The problem with North America is that we have a whole lot of perfume bottles that need to have the cork removed from the top and be poured out. We have this big stupid cork in the top of our heads. We get knocked over sometimes but we make sure nothing gets poured out. The cork is the mind. Our minds are keeping us from being poured out for Jesus. The mind and flesh are the greatest hindrance to the moving and working of God's Spirit in our lives.

God wants us to be a blessing, poured out as a drink offering around the world. Our few moments of time here on earth are not so much about what we can do for ourselves but what we can do for others.

God wants to do exciting things in all our lives, but we are afraid of being poured out. This is the only way we will be able to store up treasures in heaven. The woman that anointed Jesus, poured out all that she had. Irene would tell you that she had lived three lives; she too was willing to pour out all that she had and God took her all around the world and poured her out to many, many others.

The key is to be willing to be broken open or, to put it another way, to die to oneself. John 12:24 says "truly, truly, I say to you, unless a grain of wheat falls into the earth and dies, it will remain alone; but if it dies, it bears much fruit." The seed must go into the ground to be alone in darkness for a time, then at the right time the seed breaks open and begins to germinate, and in time it produces a plant. Soon it continues to grow into maturity, so that again at the proper time it produces fruit that will in turn be containing seeds that will in due time produce an even greater crop. One seed can produce many that in turn can produce and produce for many years to come.

In Philippians 2:17, Paul said "But even if I am being poured out as a drink offering upon the sacrifice and service of your faith, I will rejoice and share my joy with you all." This was truly Irene's life to us and to others. She was willing to be a clear bottle with the cork out. So that whosoever would come, she would pour out her Jesus into their hands and heart. How do I know that? She would be praying for nurses and doctors and for others all around her. They would observe that she was dying and in so much pain and she would say, "No I am just being poured out; I am going through the metamorphosis. I am in the cocoon stage right now, but I am breaking out for Jesus". She would ask me to pray that the Lord would release her from this cocoon. And all she asked of me was that when the day of transition and home going came, that I would be there holding her hand.

How can I speak this way so soon after my wife's passing? Because I know that my redeemer liveth and I have seen the anointing and power keep her and sustain her all through her journey with Christ, and soon and very soon I will be there in heaven too. I have been given the opportunity to take that which was poured into her life and then poured over into my life; to now pour it out into others. That is a true drink offering.

The Gospel, if poured out will go forward and revival will take place. But it will not happen until we are willing to be poured out and die. Your mind is the cork that keeps the contents from coming out. One man said the church is a lot like a pantry that is full of jars containing different preservatives. Until they are taken off the shelf and the tops screwed off and the contents poured out, the treasure inside will have no effect on anything or anyone.

The Harvest

For one to be a true disciple of Christ you must have the heart and eyes of a farmer. A farmer always looks to the harvest while he is planting and pouring out of his time and resources, having the faith and hope that in due time he will receive a harvest from that which he has planted.

God's desire for every man and woman is that they may experience the joy of bringing in a harvest both here on earth and in heaven. Christ's call is that we go out and reap where we may not have sown or watered. We reap from those who have gone before us, and others will reap from that which we have planted and leave behind as we move on in our journey home. John 4:36-38 points this out to us, *"Already he who reaps is receiving wages and is gathering fruit for life eternal; so that he who sows and he who reaps may rejoice together. For in this case the saying is true, One sows and another reaps. I sent you to reap that for which you have not laboured; others have laboured and you have entered into their labour."*

Irene was able to see this fulfilled to the point where we saw hundreds and hundreds come to know Christ as their personal Saviour in the land of Myanmar, where the famous Amidia Judson too had planted much of his family and life for Christ. We also saw over seventy-five graduate with a Diploma of Ministry from Providence, and in 2006 we will see another one hundred and thirty-five more graduate. Plus these workers are now spreading into neighbouring countries. What a joy and gift that God has given to Irene and me.

We are to be modern day harvesters. Look what the word harvest is defined as; *ingathering, reaping, crop, produce, yield, effect, fruition, produce, results, return, gather, pick, accumulate, acquire, collect, garner.*

We also have to see where we are going to invest most of our time and resources. Will it be in the area of receiving an earthly harvest or a heavenly one? Will it be storing up treasures here on earth, where at the blink of an eye they can and will be gone? Irene, when she passed on, left very few earthly treasures behind. Her focus was not on the temporal but on the eternal. She wanted to store up treasure in heaven.

I believe that not only can you store up treasure in heaven for yourself but for others also. You can place within other people treasures of God. It is not a waste of time to pour your life into someone else. The Bible says that there is no greater gift than one to lay down his life for another. John 15:13 says, "Greater love has no one than this, that one lay down his life for his friend." If you were to hear and read our personal testimony, you would find out that Irene poured herself into her friend, James Humphries, seeing the harvest potential that was there. She believed that with hard work, sacrifice and giving she would see this long haired street man turn into Doctor Humphries, who would travel the world by God's strength and fulfill God's great commission. She poured into my life all that she had, and God rewarded her by seeing fruit that has matured and lasted through all kinds of challenges and storms.

The key is to remember and keep focused as disciples on the fact that we are to be sowers and harvesters for Christ. Paul reminds the Galatians that through the Gospel and the power of the Holy Spirit they are to be responsible to keep on track and to keep going forward.

Galatians 6:7-10

"Do not be deceived, God is not mocked; for whatever a man sows, this he will also reap. For the one who sows to his own flesh will from the flesh reap corruption, but the one who sows to the spirit will from the Spirit reap eternal life. Let us not lose heart in doing good, for in due time we will reap if we do not grow weary. So then, while we have opportunity, let us do good to all people, and especially to those who are of the household of faith."

Irene did not sow to the flesh, even though for most of her life she struggled with depression and felt she was only running on three out of four cylinders. This did not hold her back from doing her best for Christ with what she was given to serve with. She sowed and harvested wherever and whenever God gave her the opportunity to do so. In much weakness of flesh she was strong in the Lord.

God in 1997 laid a verse on our heart that turned into a vision and goal for our lives. This verse became the seed bed that Project L.A.M.B.S. International was birthed from.

Matthew 9:37-38

Then He said to His disciples, "The harvest is plentiful, but the workers are few. Therefore beseech the Lord of the harvest to send out workers into His harvest."

We both felt that we must commit ourselves to training labourers and to help establish them so that they also could go out and bring in more harvest for Christ's glory.

One morning after speaking together in our home office about what God was speaking into my heart, I said to Irene, "We need to come up with a name". Irene left and after some prayer came back and said we should call it Project L.A.M.B.S., stating the word L.A.M.B.S. would be an acrostic for, Light Abroad Mobile Bible Schools. What a word from God and a vision for our lives! The first few years things were very difficult financially, but both of us felt that the call was too strong to deviate from, no matter what the cost would be.

For us to be effective as Disciples of Christ, we must see people as Christ sees them: as a harvest full of potential; a treasure that is worth dying for. The harvest is plentiful, but we must be sent out and go to where He is leading us.

Now Luke 10:1-2 states, "*Now after this the Lord appointed seventy others, and sent them in pairs ahead of Him to every city and place where He Himself was going to come." And He was saying to them, "The harvest is plentiful, but the labourers are few; therefore beseech the Lord of the harvest to send out labourers into His harvest."*

Jesus anointed the seventy to go out, and we also need to be anointed by the Holy Spirit to go out if we are going to be empowered for service. Irene knew the anointing of Christ and walked in the presence of the Holy Spirit. She knew that her flesh was temporal but the spirit was eternal. Even in the deepest hour of sickness and pain, the presence of God still flowed through her to others. We knew that we had been called to be carriers and sowers of the discipleship anointing to all who would receive.

At Christmas time 2004, she spoke the gospel of Christ, even though her body was full of cancer and pain. Then three days later she travelled to Jamaica, knowing the doctor had said to her that she might die there. Her response was that we should bury her beside her fellow student and teacher, Katie, who died two years before of similar cancer.

When we arrived in Jamaica the people were full of excitement and expectation that God had extended Irene's time, so she could come to them. One night we met with our graduates and anointed every one of them, one at a time, with oil and prayed a discipleship blessing on them. Irene wanted to see them empowered from on high so that they could go forward and serve faithfully in the body of Christ. Her dying body could not hold her back from anointing people wherever we were, on the mission field or in our home. She did not stop even in the last days in the hospital. The spirit of Christ flowed through her to others. The body did not conquer her spirit, but her spirit overcame the body, even to the last moment when she saw her fifth grandchild, Anna-Irene Prairie by video. She then knew that God was releasing her to go home.

In all that we do we must keep the vision. The focus is not on this earthly kingdom but on the Kingdom of Christ; not on my will but Christ's will, that it would be fulfilled here on earth. He told the disciples in John 4:35 *"Do you not say, there are yet four months, and then comes the harvest? Behold, I say to you, lift up your eyes and look on the fields, they are white for harvest."*

The biggest battleground that we all face is the one between the head and the heart, the struggle between our earthly nature and God's anointed Spirit. Irene saw the harvest. God allowed her to see the fields and she desired with all her heart to be a labourer in those fields. Even in the midst of great suffering her heart was burdened for those around the world. In the last days she encouraged me not to lose heart and to keep going because even though her part of the race was now coming to the end, she felt that God would release the ministry of establishing and equipping the saints into more countries. Her letter that she left me to read after she was gone states, "take courage and be strong in faith each day --- It's only a short time left, my honey, be strong, keep planting seeds while you are able.--- I know you will write and write because you have an inexhaustible amount to share. --- Just know I hope your future here will overflow with blessing."

Nothing here on earth can take away the vision that God gives, unless we ourselves relinquish it. Irene's torch burned bright until the hour of her home going.

The journey of a harvester does not come without its challenges. Hebrews 12:11 (NIV Translation) tells us, *"No discipline seems pleasant at the time, but painful. Later on, however, it produces a harvest of righteousness and peace for those who have been trained by it."*

The ministry of harvesting disciples for the Lord means that we as disciples must learn to come under discipline with our walk in Christ. You cannot mentor others until you have been mentored yourself first. The pain and suffering that Christ has promised does produce a harvest of righteousness and peace. Irene first had to be trained, and then she was able to train and equip others around the world, to bring to the lives of others in various cultures a harvest of righteousness and peace. The journey has been very challenging, but the rewards that she experienced here on earth have made it worth it all.

Finally James adds on more peace to the big picture of harvesting. James 3:17-18 (NIV Translation) *"But the wisdom that comes from heaven is first of all pure; then peace-loving, considerate, submissive, full of mercy and good fruit, impartial and sincere. Peacemakers who sow in peace raise a harvest of righteousness."*

Irene's life truly reflected all these characteristics. She walked out the word of God, some said as a princess and handmaiden of the King of Kings. Even her very name that was given by her parents means "peace". We did not know it when we married, but the name Humphries also means "peace". One could say she truly was a double portion of peace to all those she came into contact with.

Irene's investment into others was not a waste of time; it was an investment that will bring a great harvest for our family and into the church of Jesus Christ. She was and is a treasure that will keep on giving and giving.

Conclusion: Vessel of Honour

Irene did not die before her time, but she was on time.

God took her through the ultimate test to be as a vessel totally broken open and poured out for His glory. Paul told the Philippians' church, " *Brethren, I do not regard myself as having laid hold of it yet; but one thing I do: forgetting what lies behind and reaching forward to what lies ahead, I press on toward the goal for the prize of the upward call of God in Christ Jesus. (Philippians 3:13-14.)*

This was the last step of Irene's pilgrimage to press on like Paul said, for the high calling of Christ Jesus. On March 9th 2005 at 12:15 just a few hours after her 5th grandchild was born, Anna-Irene Prairie, Irene reached up and crossed over to her heavenly Father, whom she loved and missed so much, took His hand and walked into the city of our King. The race had to be completed; the line had to be crossed; the long journey was over and the time of celebration had begun.

She placed in many of us a special treasure; now what will we do with it and what will we learn from all of this? Will we be a wise steward or a foolish one? The book of James asks the question, will we just be hearers of the Word or will we be doers also? It is up to us to decide how we will choose to respond. (James 1:22-25)

Irene's life has pointed out to us four important things that each disciple of Christ must keep focused on if he or she is going to experience fruit that will last from their labours. One is to remember that we are just in a temporary vessel that God works through to bless and minister to others. Secondly that in that vessel is a great treasure of immense value. Thirdly, before that treasure can be a blessing and a help to others, it has to be poured out. And last of all God has given to us a great harvest field for us to have value and purpose in, for us to reap great rewards and blessings from.

Paul tells Timothy about vessels of honour. He states, *"Now in a large house there are not only gold and silver vessels, but also vessels of wood and earthenware, and some to honour and some to dishonour. Therefore, if anyone cleans himself from these things, he will be a* ***vessel of honour****, sanctified, useful to the Master, prepared for every good work."* (II Timothy 2:20-21)

Irene has quietly blazed a trail that has pointed upward to Jesus Christ. She has been useful in the Masters hands. On behalf of the family of God, we say, "well done thou good and faithful servant".

Even though Irene has moved on, her life will still be producing fruit here on earth long after she has been gone, because she has planted good seeds that will keep producing fruit here on earth and in heaven for many years to come.

Thank you so much, Irene, for being a vessel in our midst and around the world.

P.S. From the heart of your manservant Jim, Irene. May God be praised and glorified!

CHAPTER TWO

Family Tributes

Thirty-three years ago Irene began the long process of discipling me and making me into who I am in Christ today. Right from the beginning she always believed that God was going to do something special in my life and that she wanted to be part of it. She in a very loving and encouraging way mentored and moulded me as a disciple of Christ.

There were at least two key areas that she taught to me over and over again, almost everyday of her life. One was on an area of grace and forgiveness and the second was on having a clear personal relationship with Christ Jesus.

I was a hippy and then became a Jesus freak, but she saw through all the outer trappings and looked past all the terrible things that I had done in the past. Six weeks after meeting we decided it would be easier to serve the Lord together so on July 8th we were married.

I started pastoring when I was nineteen years old and she was the one that taught me how to study the Word of God and how to prepare sermons for Sunday. After four years of the pastorate, she patiently encouraged me to go to Bible School and get my BRE. Then go on to get my Masters degree and finally my Doctorate. She did all the typing and spell-check and grammar repair and correction. She never gave up on me but stuck to the vision that she had told me about before we were married.

Then in the last few years of her life I was able to help her somewhat to get her Masters degree. In reality all the degrees that I have, she should have received because she was the woman of great faith and vision that encouraged me to keep going forward.

Then in 1996 I shared with her that I believed God was changing somewhat the direction of our ministry from pastoring to discipleship training. With great faith and sacrifice we stepped out hand and hand and Project L.A.M.B.S. International was birthed forth. Again she laboured long hours in writing and helping to lay out at least twenty-four courses that would be taught around the world.

I had the privilege of seeing Jesus in her life each day and I saw first hand what it meant to be a servant of the Lord Jesus Christ. I knew Jesus was real and living because I met Him each day in the life of Irene.

Now she has completed her race and has passed the torch on to me so that in turn I would pass the disciple equipping and training vision on to others, as the Lord gives to me strength and time.

She poured into me a treasure that had been given to her by God. I have and will continue to be the fruit that she trusted and believed God would keep on using for His glory. Thank you Irene, I will always be indebted to you and to Christ for helping me to see and understand what true living and freedom was all about.

Your friend and manservant,
James

James Humphries - Husband

"Earth has no sorrow that Heaven cannot heal" (Moore)

I know that my mother is with her Maker and is also surrounded by everyone she loves; that have gone on before her. My Mom's life was nothing short of a testimony to the world she lived in.

All those that time spent with my Mother were drawn to her unbelievable ways of showing love. As her son, I really didn't and don't understand the scope, but my Mother truly loved life and everyone with an ability to look through the bad and even the evil to see the good.

There are countless times that she would go beyond what a good citizen, a good friend, a good sister, a good mother, and a good Christian would do. What brings peace to me is seeing just how alive this love is in all the people that carry a piece of it. Her only wish would be to share this love with others.

P.S. Mom, it won't be long. Save us a few seats up front!

Love Ya!

Josh Humphries
& Family

Josh Humphries - Son

To my dearest Mother,

... You are the glue that has kept this family together. It is because of you that I love my family so much. I feel like I have not had enough time and that Andi, Jeremy, and Tyah haven't had enough time. I know I am so lucky to have had so much time with you. I know you as a person and friend, not just as my mother.

You are kind, loving, generous and a wonderful grandparent. I hope you know how much I love you and cherish our relationship.

I want you to know how thankful I am for all your support over the years. Things were not always easy. And we didn't always see eye to eye, but I never doubted your friendship and support. Thank you for that. I hope you will be comforted to know that you have been the <u>most</u> important person in my life. You have contributed more to my life and the kid's life than anyone.

Well, I really can't go on; it's too hard to write all this down. I just wanted you to know how important you have been, and are to me. I love you so much. I will always have such good memories of our times together. These I will tell Tyah, so she can know what a wonderful woman, mother, and grandmother she has. I will do my best to tell her all I can so she can look up to you like Andi and I do. I want her to know you like we do. I will try to not think about what we are missing, but what we have shared.

I love you; I hope you know what you mean to me and everyone around you.

I love you,
Your daughter Rachel

Rachel Amoah-Gyampoh - Daughter* This was a portion of a letter that was written by Rachel a few weeks before Irene's home going. Irene had me read it to her several times a day and drew much strength from it.

Grandma always watched over me and listened to what I had to say. She was awesome! There is one moment I always treasured. It was when we used to sleep in her bed together, and Grandpa would go to sleep with Jeremy, and Grandma would tell me the story of Snowflake and how he got lost and how the shepherd went to find the little sheep. After Grandma told me that story she told me the one about Esther. When we finished that, we prayed for a good night's sleep. Then we did a muscle exercise – first you would start at your head and then got to your feet. You would hold your head to your shoulders and then squeeze. Then you squeeze your hands together and hold and you would do that with as many parts of your body as you could. Then we would go to sleep.

We would wake up in the morning, go downstairs and make cream of wheat for Breakfast. And whenever I made it Grandma said there were no lumps and she would say it was very good!

This is what I loved to do with my Grandma when I slept over.

Love, Andi

Andi Hiebert – Granddaughter

CHAPTER THREE

World Wide Tributes & Reflections - LETTERS

Irene Humphries – Reminiscence

I first encountered Irene when her husband Jim began as a student in the Providence Seminary Doctor of Ministry program, where I served as Academic Vice-President. My initial impression was of a quiet and somewhat shy woman who was (as I termed it) a "typical pastors wife." It would not be long before I realized how deceiving first impressions can be.

As I got to know Jim and Irene better, I became aware that Irene was a person in her own right, and not just an adjunct of her husband. She had a vision for where Christ wanted to take her, and how she would prepare herself to carry that vision out. As a result, it was not long before her application for admissions to the Master of Arts in Global Christian Studies crossed my desk. By this time, I was much better acquainted with Irene, and there was no question in my mind that what she set out to do, she would accomplish. It was a pleasure to have her as one of our students (I have always been in favour of mature and godly students!). It soon became obvious that she was highly intelligent and perceptive in her outlook and work.

As the vision of L.A.M.B.S. took shape in Jim's mind and we met together to discuss it, Irene was often a part of the conversation. I was impressed by her passion for Third World peoples and their salvation. I was even more impressed by her determination to be a part of Christ's solution to their dilemma.

In 1998, I got to see Irene in action, when I was invited, as Academic Vice-President of Providence Seminary, to be speaker at the first L.A.M.B.S. graduation ceremony of their school in Ewarton, Jamaica. Irene, Jim, and I flew down for a week of worship, teaching, and celebration. It was clear that the Jamaican people of the churches and school in Ewarton loved Irene immensely. It was also demonstrated in their ordination of her as a minister in the Independent Assemblies of God of Jamaica. The service was one in which the Spirit of God was unquestionably present.

When I was made aware of the invasion of Irene's body by cancer, once again her demeanour of deep accepting faith that whatever God would do was what she desired, I found overwhelming. And when the cancer went into remission, we all rejoiced that God had answered our prayers.

Shortly after that, my wife and I moved to Cambridge, Ontario where I became Executive Vice-President and Seminary Dean of Heritage College and Seminary. When Jim and Irene visited, it was old home week! And then came the terrible news that the cancer was back—but once more, it was evident from Irene's newsletters that she was prepared to accept whatever God had in store, even if it meant her life. What a witness!

Since her death, I have reflected upon Irene's life and faith. Why did God call her home? That is one of those questions unanswerable this side of heaven. I like to think that He had a task for her to perform in that sphere for His glory. My prayer would be that I would have a similar faith that calmly accepts and thanks God for whatever He sends my way.

David Smith – Executive Vice President & Academic Dean of Heritage Bible College – Guelph, Ontario

Wholehearted ministry and devotion

She came into my office with a look of wonderment and said, "Chuck, what am I doing here at Providence Seminary? I am a grandmother who has been out school for years." However, the determination that she had proved that she not only belonged at Providence, but that she was an outstanding student and servant of God. That, of course, was Irene; what she did, she did wholeheartedly to the Lord.

When I think of Irene (meaning peaceful, and she was), I feel that her name could also be changed to Ruth (meaning friend) without any difficulty. As one looks at the character of Ruth, you cannot help but see Irene. In Chapter one, Ruth had RESOLVE, when she determined to do something she did it. That was Irene; she too showed a determined spirit. Chapter two shows Ruth's UNSELFISHNESS as she ministered to her mother-in-law and carried out her duties faithfully. Again Irene stands out in this area. She was always ready to serve and give. Ruth's TRUST is evident in Chapter three. She trusted her mother-in-law, Boaz and most of all God. There's Irene, showing childlike trust in her Lord first, then her husband, Jim, and finally in others as she sought wisdom and discernment. Like Ruth in Chapter four, Irene received HONOR. She was recognized by Providence for her outstanding work as a student. Many other groups also recognized her for her hard work and dedication. She received honour from her family, but most of all she is now enjoying the honour given by her Lord with a "well done, you good and faithful servant."

Susan and I had the privilege of knowing Irene as a friend (Ruth). Her dedication to God was and is an inspiration. She truly had a life of wholehearted ministry and devotion to her Lord.

Chuck Nichols – Professor of Educational Ministries at Providence Theological Seminary, also Board Chairman of Project L.A.M.B.S. International Inc., Steinbach, Manitoba

There she was again. That feminine little Baptist girl. When she would pass in the hall at Arthur Voaden Secondary School, I was too shy to really look directly at her, but I could feel that gentle smile. A soft greeting, "Hi Bob", "Hi Irene". I don't remember how I knew her, but I just knew she was one of the purest followers of Jesus that I had ever met.

She was very quiet, yet you could hear her life speak as she sometimes sat alone in the high school cafeteria. She was petite, pretty, and had a wonderful personality, but her testimony was so pure that there were times I felt I wasn't even worthy to sit with her because it might tarnish her reputation. She never boasted, or even lifted her voice, but it is like everyone knew she was pure. She would never condemn anyone, yet the light of Jesus in her would make you aware of the darkness in yourself.

It was at an evening meal in 1972, at Wayside Inn, Talbotville, Ontario, where Karen, my wife and I were dining, over at another table was Irene and her good friend Brenda. They were so excited about what was happening among the "hippies". Irene felt something had to be done to provide a place to disciple these wild new Christians. We invited Irene and Brenda over to our apartment, and after a time of sharing and prayer, the vision to establish a drop-in center, coffee shop was born.

We started "The Fountain", a coffeehouse week nights, complete with "Kids Bible Club" on Saturday mornings. (Irene always carried a burden to give the gospel to children.) If I remember right, over one hundred young people came to faith in Christ that summer. We had tent meetings downtown, water baptisms at Port Stanley and in Pineafore Park Pond, nightly Bible Studies complete with genuine exorcisms, and hungry new believers receiving the fullness of the Holy Spirit. Somehow in all the chaos, Irene was the person who represented a sense of quiet, peaceful confidence that God was definitely in control.

Then it happened. We were doing some afternoon street witnessing when quiet Irene came running up to me quite out of breath with excitement, "I am going to marry Jim Humphries", she exclaimed. My thoughts were, "You're what? Not Jimmer! Why he is just a new Christian, and … well he has been one of the main drug dealers in town… and he is from such an unstable family… and you are so innocent and pure… and naïve. How could this be happening?" It seemed before you could plan a wedding they were marching down the aisle, out of the church and into our Rambler, (an extinct model of car today) and off on their honeymoon.

Jim and Irene moved into an apartment over the coffeehouse and we all moved right in with them. It was a pioneer House Church. It was just so natural. Irene, that sweet innocent Baptist girl, had longed for the infilling of the Holy Spirit for so long. Others received a prayer language so easy, yet it almost seemed it wasn't for Irene. One day a preaching brother (I believe Brother Day) stopped by the ministry office where Irene worked and after a brief conversation where she explained that she wanted the Baptism of the Holy Spirit; he without hesitation prayed for her to receive the Holy Spirit, and proceeded to thank the Lord for baptizing her. She asked him how she could be baptized without speaking in a heavenly language, and he just told her, "Oh you will, you will".

One evening not long after that we were gathered at Jim and Irene's for a Bible Study that went fairly late, so Irene graciously excused herself and went to bed for the night. A while later we heard some unusual sounds coming from the rear of the apartment. And so Jim went to check if the cats were fighting or something. That sound turned out to be Irene. Thinking she would give a few words of thanksgiving to the Lord before she went to sleep, instead she experienced a full release of the precious Holy Spirit within her. Quiet Irene wasn't quiet that night. What a joy to know that she was joyously filled without the question of "Did someone influence her? Was she just worked up into some emotional fever?" No, the Lord so wonderfully sensitive to Irene released her baptism to her in such a private manner, yet with a host of witnesses near by. It was so Holy Spirit, and so Irene.

Irene remained true to her love of the Word of God, yet became a woman led by the Holy Spirit

Irene was small in stature but mighty in passion for souls, especially children. Just like she fired up Karen and I to start the coffeehouse, now she had Jimmer to work on. The next thing I knew Jim and Irene were roller brush painting a school bus that had been donated to them by the Salvation Army, (and when the Salvation Army is through with a bus, it's had better days). They were off to Port Stanley to start a mobile Kids Club in the bus which was minus a front seat or two to set up the keyboard and easel. Their outreach was so successful they moved to a winterized cottage as their home in Port Stanley, and opened a condemned scout hall for planting a full-blown church. At this point, they asked Karen and me to join them in establishing this new work.

I must say Jim sure matured through the next years, and I'm sure having a live-in Bible teacher wife sped up the process. One day Jim came to me to say that the Lord had confirmed to him and Irene that he should go to seminary to prepare for a life of ministry. Hard to believe that this, hair to the waist, drinking, drug dealer had married a princess bride and been transformed into a seminary student. There must have been a secret kiss somewhere! She believed in him; that was for sure. Off they moved to Saskatchewan, family in tow, and we kept in touch over the years.

I know that Jim and Irene experienced many blessings from the Lord, but I must say it seemed that this innocent Baptist girl had more than her share of trials in life. I guess having radical surgery for cancer was just one of those trials, but whenever we would meet, somehow she would always be smiling, and those big dark eyes always seemed to have a twinkle of praise for the Lord. It is just hard to understand why someone so peaceful and pure was chosen to suffer so much.

The scripture in 2 Corinthians: 7-9 describes Irene so well. *"But we have this treasure in jars of clay to show that this all-surpassing power is from God and not from us. We are hard pressed on every side, but not crushed; perplexed, but not in despair; persecuted, but not abandoned; struck down, but not destroyed."*

It seems Irene's life was indeed pressed in on every side; family, health, ministry, relationships; at times perplexed by why things happened as they did; persecuted relentlessly by disease; and finally knocked down…but her spirit was never crushed, she never gave up in despair, she never claimed the Lord abandoned her, and though her body was knocked down, Irene was never destroyed. I'm sure anyone who knows her would say this is true.

It's like Irene carried death around in her body for years, so that all of us could see the resurrection life of Jesus in her. It had to be the all-surpassing power of God that we were hearing in her voice, and the light of the glory of Christ we were looking at in those eyes. Yes, we could see her body was just clay, but it was lined with the purest gold.

Writing this tribute has been a wonderful experience for me. I've relived many memories, so many more than I could share. It makes me want to be like the Jesus I saw and knew in Irene.

"Oh Lord, we who are still alive are always given over to death for Your sake, so that Your life may be revealed in our body.

We know oh Father that it was You who raised our Lord Jesus from the dead, and You will raise us with Jesus to be with You in Your presence forever. We do not lose heart. Though our bodies are wasting away may our spirits be renewed day by day. We know that our painful trials here are relatively light and momentary compared to the eternal glory that we will live in.

Dear Lord, help us in our trial to be like Irene and fix our eyes not on what is seen, but on what is unseen and eternal. Lord what we do with each day is of utmost importance, because we will exchange a day of our life for it. Lord, Irene lived her life unselfishly for others, and by serving them with a sacrificial life demonstrated her love for You. Irene finished her race for You. You were the one all the time that she desired to please. It is now Your face that she looks upon, and it is You who now look into her eyes. Oh Lord, let her life continue to inspire each of us to forget what is behind, look unto You, and run the race into Your waiting arms. Amen."

Bob & Karen Gal - Former Senior Pastor in Edmonton, Alberta. Bob was a groom's man at our wedding. He also was a deacon at Jim and Irene's first pastorate in Port Stanley Ontario.

In loving memory of our first secretary Irene-Humphries-Haight

When God called me to start helping those who were suffering so much for the cause of Christ in Communist controlled countries, I was a young mother of three children, living with my husband Klaas in St. Thomas, Ontario.

My heart was awakened to the plight of these martyrs by the Holy Spirit who used Pastor Richard Wurmbrand's testimonies from behind the Iron Curtain to impress upon me the great need of lifting these brothers and sisters in Christ up in prayer and at the same time find ways and means to come to their aid. The year was 1974.

God's call came unmistakably and I knew that if I would not heed that call, I would let a great opportunity pass. For a while I let fear get into my heart, but when I did that the peace of God left me. There is nothing worse than when God turns his back on you – life no longer has the same meaning. After I asked God to forgive me for my doubts and fears, I received His peace once again. My husband Klaas also heeded God's call and joined the Mission two years later.

After getting a crash course in how to set up the Mission "Jesus to the Communist World Inc." in 1974, God provided me with a loving, caring babysitter who would also be my secretary for half days. This was Irene Haight. Our children immediately took to Irene – they loved her. Today they still say that she was our best babysitter. When I would come home at twelve noon, Irene would go to the office and do whatever she could find to do. She was a blessing sent by God. When Irene met her future husband Jim and had her wedding date set after a few months, we had the privilege of attending their wedding with our family. We felt blessed because we saw Irene so happy. We knew that these two would from now on walk with the Lord and that their future would be safe in His hands. When their first child, Joshua, was born they handed out New Testaments to family, friends and acquaintances. (See Picture below).

We thank God for the rich blessing Irene has been to our family and to the Mission as well. We saw Love in its highest form in her whole demeanour. We look forward to meeting her again soon.

Mrs. Nellie Brobbel
Voice of the Martyrs Inc.
Canada

Mrs. Nellie Brobbel - co-founder of Voice of the Martyrs of Canada

IRENE HUMPRHIES

The relationship my family and I had with Irene was not full of countless memories nor did it span numerous decades, but it did impact our lives in a way that changed us for the better.

We experienced through observation and relationship, what Gods' grace looks like in another persons life, miracles of healing as well as love that can only be expressed in that way when a person is saturated with the Spirit of God.

We met Jim and Irene through the leading of the Lord to study and prepare for ministry via Project L.A.M.B.S. Both Jim and Irene confirmed to us that God's call was on our lives for ministry and took a personal interest in our lives that involved more than just words.

Through study I encountered many new doctrinal and theological stumbling blocks that caused me to seriously seek and ask questions that had not challenged me prior to school. When Jim told Irene of my struggles and questions, she immediately requested that Dallas (my wife) and I come to their home in Marchand so she could share her experiences with us as well as encourage and pray for us. Her immediate response was to care for my spiritual condition and future as well as to do her part to disciple me. This is the fundamental foundation on which Project L.A.M.B.S. International is built and Irene lived as a part of her life. She did not make it an 8 AM to 5 PM ministry, she was willing to sacrifice her personal time and space on many occasions to ensure that she was doing her part to help people to understand the grace and unending love of the One for whom she was a zealous ambassador.

Numerous times while attempting to minister to Irene during her battle with cancer she would turn the tables on you and you would find her ministering to you instead. One such instance that was a cut above the rest happened on a Thursday evening. Earlier in the day, Irene's pains had been out of control and situations arose that brought her within inches of the end of her life. She had been put on a morphine pump and was not in good shape at all. I had agreed earlier in the week to go with my friend Glenn Wiebe to help Jim put up some drywall in the new addition. When we arrived Jim was in pretty rough shape emotionally due to the events of the day and informed us of Irene's condition. As we worked on the room, I asked Jim if I could go up and sing for her after we finished. Jim asked her and she invited us up. After some conversation, I sang "The calmer of the storm" for her. What we experienced next was a true miracle, Irene stood up off the sofa where she had been lying and asked if she could pray for the three of us. She took a bottle of anointing oil and anointed Jim, Glenn and myself and prayed for each one of us with boldness and clarity. Jim informed me later that the doctors said the amount of morphine she was taking was enough to take all of our lives in the room that night. After praying for us, she requested that we all go downstairs so she could see the drywall work we had done. Jim was very hesitant due to the fact she had not been downstairs in days. She behaved as if she was completely healed for the time. She walked down the stairs on her own, checked out the work, blessed our socks off and encouraged us until the minute we left. There was no shortage of the Spirit of the living God in the Humphries home!!!!

During the last few days of her life I was able to visit with her in the hospital and to again sing for her at her bedside. Even in that condition her love for her God and for people still shone as radiantly as the sun on a clear July afternoon. Her sense of humour and wit were still intact and she made every effort to use them and to bless me right to the end.

Although my time with Irene was short in comparison to many that knew her, she had a profound impact in my life, as well as in life of my wife and children. She went out of her way to bless Dallas and each one of my children, paying special attention to our daughter, Amy.

There are numerous stories that can be told about this woman of faith but they will all relate the same message. Irene Humphries cared more for the personal and spiritual well being of the people than the majority of the people in this nation. She reflected the truth of what it means to "Love the Lord your God with all your heart, soul, mind and strength" and "To love your neighbour as yourself."

Irene Humphries was truly Jesus with skin on to our family and it was a pleasure to have had the opportunity to share in her life and to be blessed with the amount of time and experiences that God made available to us.

May God be glorified through her life and the telling of these stories!

Thank you,
Darcy Brown

Darcy Brown - Project L.A.M.B.S. and Project Shepherds Student in Steinbach, MB.

A Tribute to Irene

The first time I met Irene, she and Jim were visiting my home church, presenting a Project L.A.M.B.S. report. I remember glancing over at Irene from across the sanctuary and thinking how graceful, beautiful and ladylike she appeared. I came to learn, in the years that followed, that she was all of those and so much more.

Irene played many roles in my life as I worked alongside her and Jim at Project L.A.M.B.S. First as a teacher, I marvelled as she taught a class in the study of Romans. She was seemingly quiet and reserved before I saw her step up to the pulpit. There, she glowed as she beautifully explained God's righteousness and grace, and their power in our lives. Her passion for God was so obvious as she spoke, and it made her class a delight.

In the office, Irene taught me some artistic tricks in putting together eye catching displays and newsletters. She made it look so easy by using her creativity and artistry, and the perfectionist in her also came out as we would fuss over small details, sometimes for hours, until it met her satisfaction. She taught me the importance of paying attention to detail.

Another role Irene played in my heart was that of a dear friend. As we would walk during our lunch breaks, she admired and appreciated God's work in creation around us, and I felt safe to share with her a struggle I was going through, something God was teaching me, or challenges I had. Wherever we would share, be it on the veranda in Marchand or on the veranda in Jamaica, Irene always offered a listening ear and an honest response that was never judgemental. Even if it was something I didn't want to hear, I knew that what she was sharing was spoken gently from her heart and backed up in much prayer. She was a true friend.

Irene took her role of being a mother seriously, and because of the amount of time we spent together, I soon felt like part of the family. Irene shared her kitchen and some cooking secrets with me, but what sticks with me to this day was her devotion and love for her family. She shared her husband's vision for discipleship as they pursued God wholeheartedly. And she reserved a very special place for her children in her heart. I remember as we'd be working in the office and she'd receive a phone call from either Rachel or Josh, often she would drop whatever she was doing and pray for them.

Graceful, beautiful and ladylike all well describe Irene outwardly. Inwardly, I saw a woman of prayer, devotion, and sincerely in love with Jesus. She set an example for all of us to follow as a disciple of Jesus, and I can't wait to rejoice with her at His throne someday soon!

Allison McDonald – Former Secretary & Missionary with Project L.A.M.B.S. International Inc. – Present Canadian Director of Project L.A.M.B.S. School in Jamaica together with her husband Bert McDonald.

How does someone adequately give honour to another who has been a faithful servant for the LORD? This is the daunting task that our dear friend, Dr. James (Jim) Humphries has taken on for his precious wife, Beatrice Irene Humphries.

Sharon and my link in her life goes back to 1986 when we had the privilege to work with Jim and Irene in Fort McMurray, AB. Jim was the Senior Pastor and I was asked to serve as their Minister of Christian Education. This gave us plenty of opportunity to see this couple in action.

It was during that early time that the church decided to expand their sanctuary and CE wing. Here is where one of the many gifts of Irene came to my notice. She had a unique understanding for colours and decorating. Her special creative "touches" were enjoyed by many of us for years. I will always be proud of the sanctuary where she placed her special touch.

Her artistic and creative talents were not only limited to decor. She was also a "budding" writer (especially poetry). The way that she could express herself made you feel right at home while reading her penned words. Yet most of her talent was hidden in those years.

Many times we received "little notes" of encouragement from our "Barnabas-like sister." She had that unique, gentle, compassionate, sensitivity to recognize when someone needed a "little help from a friend" and ministered with the Holy Ghost's guidance. Our children will never forget the fairness and non-judgemental attitude of Irene. Irene genuinely loved them "where they were at."

Josh and Rachel were in their adolescent years during their time up north. Irene always seemed to be able to calmly walk through the "teen" challenges that this brings to parenthood. She was a great example to our wives and mothers who were walking through similar challenges.

Irene stood on her own even though she probably would argue with me (gently) about my conclusion. Yet I've watched her stand as God's spokeswoman and receiving the admiration that she rightly deserved. But God chose to not have her stand alone. In His wisdom he made an incredible team of husband and wife, mother and father, grandfather and grandmother to more than just their natural offspring.

After spending time with Jim and Irene teaching with Project L.A.M.B.S, I gained a newer appreciation of Irene. She could teach God's Word (the Book of Romans) with a sincerity and gentleness that I greatly appreciated. Not many, along my journey of life, have had this kind of spirit in their teaching. I can still remember a sermon she spoke in McMurray on the "Faith Chapter." That is unique with me because I can't say I can remember many sermons – even most of the ones I've preached!

I came to see this precious woman of God reach her point of maturity before God chose to take her to her reward. I've often wondered about God's timing, yet I know He always does what is best. He gives and he takes away - blessed be His name. God birthed a seed in Irene that grew to become a princess to all those who were blessed to know her.

I thank God for the times our lives crossed. Knowing the Humphries has enriched our lives. May God give me the same faith and stamina to stand up against the many trials of life that seem to increase as we reach our final destination.

Pastor Brad & Sharon Montsion - Fellow Pastor in Fort McMurray, Alberta. Teacher for Project L.A.M.B.S. and Senior Pastor of Fountaingate Christian Assembly.

I first met Irene some twenty-nine years ago when she and her husband Jim were preaching in Ste. Anne, but I only got to really know her the last five years, and especially the last two and a half years before she passed away.

Irene was a very special lady and what a privilege it was to have known her. She was a princess, and that's what I called her "Princess", and that's because that is what she reminded me of. She was beautiful inside and out.

Irene was a very thankful person, first and foremost thankful to God for His goodness and His grace in her life. It was through the many trials and challenges in her life that she truly came to experience and to understand God's grace. She was thankful for her husband Jim, her "manservant" as she called him, who sacrificially devoted himself to her care during her battle with cancer. She was thankful for her children and grandchildren, and she loved them so much. She was very grateful to God for all her friends and church family; all the support she received through prayer, words of encouragement, cards, e-mails, flowers, gifts, and meals was not taken for granted. She appreciated every caring gesture; the outpouring of love sometimes was almost more than she could take, and she likened it to a "giant going-away party". She was also thankful to all the doctors, nurses and home care staff who diligently devoted themselves to her care.

Irene was also a very thoughtful and considerate person; she always wanted to make sure that those she loved knew they were appreciated. She loved to send cards and notes. Even when she was sick, she was considerate to ask how you were doing.

Most of all, Irene was a devoted servant of the Lord, having a passion to see others come to Jesus and walk in the righteousness of God. She had a heart for the nations, - for Jamaica, Myanmar, Africa and more. She loved the Word of God; she never missed an opportunity to preach or teach or share a word of testimony. She was faithful to God's calling in her life. She was a woman of prayer; she believed in a God who answers prayer. She desired nothing more than to be in the perfect will of God and her desire was to glorify Him no matter what circumstances came her way. She suffered much but her faith in God never wavered; as she remained steadfast and focused on the Lord till the very end, she experienced His peace. We could say that she lived up to the full meaning of her name: --Irene means "Peace".

Irene leaves behind a wonderful legacy of love, of faith in God, of courage, of steadfastness in the midst of trials and suffering. Her life will always remain a testimony of the grace of God. She was a wonderful example to me personally and to so many and she will be sadly missed. Till we meet again, dear friend!

Louise Broesky - Friend, Student and former Secretary with Project L.A.M.B.S. International Inc. She spent many hours walking closely with Irene in the last part of her Pilgrimage.

A Tribute to Pastor Irene Humphries

I do not remember the day or the year when I had my first conversation with Sister Irene. But I do remember the location, which was just south of Steinbach where the Humphries had rented a machine shop at the time in which they were building portable signs. When I asked Irene how she felt about their new business, she hesitantly replied, "I hope this is only a temporary thing. Jim and I are praying that God will open a new door of opportunity for us to get back into the ministry." As our conversation continued I soon realized that there was a deep desire in this woman's heart to be full-time in the ministry.

Well, the good Lord answered their prayers, and once again Jim and Irene were back in the ministry. As her pastor, I had the privilege of going on a ministry trip to the Ukraine together with Pastor Irene and her husband Dr. Jim, where Irene taught the women during the day and also shared at our evangelistic crusades during the evenings. And I sensed that her ministry was greatly appreciated by the people in the Ukraine. And as elsewhere, Sister Irene was always greatly respected whenever she shared or taught or preached a message.

Although Pastor Irene's life on earth was short, yet she has been a tremendous influence and a great testimony not only in her ministry but also in her suffering and struggles with cancer. She deeply loved the Lord and was also deeply devoted to Him and the ministry He had given her. Sister Irene will be remembered by many as one who was fully committed and willing to serve wherever the Lord directed her. Her desire to be an effective servant was also revealed in the sacrifices she made in order to graduate from Bible College. Sister Irene was not only a great individual person, but also a great team-mate. That is one of the reasons her husband Dr. Jim has been as successful in his ministry as he is today. Because she played a great part in birthing Project L.A.M.B.S. and to carry it through it's birthing struggles.

I personally count it a "great blessing" to have had the opportunity of ministering together, praying together, and weeping together with Pastor Irene and her husband Dr. Jim. And ever since I began to know them, they have been two special people in my life. My relationship with Irene was not only that of a pastor to one of his parishioners, but it was also a father to daughter and daughter to father relationship. Ever since Irene lost her parents, I sensed that I had become somewhat of a father figure to her.

Sister & Pastor Irene was a great person who has touched many lives in different countries around the world. She was also a great blessing to her home church, Gospel Chapel, where many of the members were greatly encouraged by her ministry and her heart stirring testimonies. Pastor Irene was a saint to the ends degree. And will always be remembered as such.

But the good Lord has taken her home to receive her reward. Although we on earth wept, the angels in heaven rejoiced when this dear saint came through the pearly gates to forever be free from all the pain and suffering she endured here on earth. Because, "God will wipe away every tear from (her) eyes; there shall be no more pain, for the former things have passed away." (Rev. 2:4) And, "Blessed are the dead who die in the Lord from now on. "Yes," says the Spirit that they may rest from their labours, and their works follow them." (Rev. 14:13)

Will see you there soon.

Pastor Peter Broesky - Pastor of our Home Church in La Broquerie, Foundational Board Advisor to Project L.A.M.B.S. International Inc., and a teacher in this ministry.

The Lord sent Irene into my life when I was going through a most difficult time. The Humphries family moved into a house across the street from us. I went to introduce myself and welcome them into the community and Irene and me connected. I sensed such a love for Jesus in her and I was at a point where I wanted to grow in my relationship with the Lord. I just knew that this woman would be a positive person in my life. This was the beginning of our journey together and we remained dear friends until the Lord chose to take her home. We were kindred spirits. She was always there for me and I will always treasure that.

One of the things that stick out in my mind so much was her passion for prayer. This is also a passion of mine and so whenever we would see each other we always took time to pray. She gave me this book, 'Prayer Changes Things' many years ago and I still use it from time to time even now.

We loved to walk and our conversations would always revolve around the Lord, about His goodness and mercy and faithfulness and the importance of giving all our burdens to the King of Kings and Lord of Lords.

Irene was a lady with many talents. The year my husband Dennis and me celebrated our 25th anniversary, she more or less did all the work for me. I don't have the creative ideas, but she came up with a plan and together with Jim's skills as carpenter, we made a beautiful backdrop to be used in the back of our head table. Our whole day was really special and it was due to her God-given talents, and her willingness to bless me. During the preparations for this day we spent time in Winnipeg and had a blast shopping and doing lunch.

There were times in our lives when we didn't see each other for awhile, but when we connected again it was as though we never missed a beat. We enjoyed each other's company.

I remember the time Jim had given her this little MGB, and we went cruising to Winnipeg for supper one night. The top was down and it was a beautiful night and we just had a great time letting down our hair a little and enjoying the great outdoors. We also had a little excursion up to Flin Flon. Our son, Lyle, needed a ride up there for his work and she agreed to come for the ride. I was grateful that she came so that I didn't have to drive that distance back by myself. We took the scenic route and stopped at Clear Lake and just enjoyed the beauty of Manitoba. It was a great drive and we treasured our time together.

Jim and Irene did a lot of traveling and I treasure all the different things that she has brought me from other countries. They have a special place in my home.

I remember the stories that she used to write at Christmas time and they'd be published in the Carillon Christmas edition and I was always eager to see what she had written. She was so crafty; it was amazing the decorations she'd come up with for the Travelodge Hotel and the vet clinic in Winnipeg, plus all her input at church.

I marvelled at her academic skills. I was so happy for her and so proud of her when she graduated with her Master of Arts from Providence. Her graduating was a great accomplishment for her even though at times she would tell me how tired she was. She was a determined lady and when she made up her mind to do something she followed through with it. I so admired that in her.

They moved to Fort McMurray for a few years and I remember going to see them and they took us to the Tar Sands. It was a real learning experience for us. This trip to see them was a wonderful memory for me. It was good news to me when she informed me that they were moving back to good old Manitoba.

It was devastating to me and everybody else when she was diagnosed with cancer and I was amazed at her fighting spirit. She truly wanted to beat this thing and the Lord did give her a miracle and He gave her extra time. We were all grateful for that...she really fought the fight with grace and dignity.

Irene always thought of others and even when she was in a lot of pain and discomfort she would inquire about my family and how they were doing. The time I spent with her during the last two and a half years and the many prayers we lifted up to our Heavenly Father will forever be etched in my memories of my dear friend Irene. Our last walk together here on this earth was last year when she managed to complete the Pallative Care Walk. We shared with each other about the joy it will be when we walk the golden streets of Heaven. There will be no pain there and we'll walk, run or jog to our hearts content. A few days before she went home to be with the Lord, my husband and I went to see her and it was a very precious time as the four of us had the opportunity to sing and pray together one more time.

What a day it will be, when we will see each other again. Thanks for the memories my dear friend.

Hilda Martin - Long time close friend, encourager and helper to Irene.

A TRIBUTE FOR IRENE HUMPHRIES

It is a great honour to write a tribute on behalf of Irene Humphries, a very true friend and colleague in the ministry of our Lord Jesus Christ.

I first met Irene just over 40 years ago upon my becoming her pastor. She was a beautiful, compassionate, loving and considerate young woman, very endearing qualities, which she retained until the time of her death. It was in 1972 that Jim Humphries (now Dr. James Humphries) came to St. Thomas. No one could have imagined then what great things God would do for and through them.

Jim was soundly converted, Irene was already a Christian and they were married in 1972. If ever the term "helpmeet" could be applied to a wife, it certainly describes Irene Humphries.

Immediately, she and Jim launched into ministries; coffee houses were established, ministering to people the churches weren't touching. Irene's loving and gracious manner naturally won over some of the apparently most hardened.

They went on to Briercrest Bible College and from there God called them to pastoral work. Wherever they were, God so gifted them, they were able to win men, women, and young people to Jesus Christ.

Over the last few years, Irene worked and received her Masters degree while Jim has earned his doctorate from Providence College. Also, directed by the Holy Spirit, they founded the excellent Ministry of Project L.A.M.B.S. International Inc. from which many pastors who could not otherwise afford training have benefited, and through those pastors uncounted hundreds of God's people. This whole ministry was a joint project of Jim and Irene.

In the midst of all this, she was also a loving, biblical mother to Joshua and Rachel.

God has called Irene to Him to glory after an illness, which she bore with great fortitude. Modest and unassuming she would consider herself unworthy of the tributes that have flowed in, but she was and is indeed a great woman of God, an inspiration and example to many of us who can say that we are proud and thankful to have known Irene Humphries.

Written by Pastor Donald Fitchett

Pastor Don was the Pastor who married Irene and I on July 8, 1972. He has faithfully walked with us and has been a true testimony to us; that we have tried to pattern our lives after. He is an ordained minister with the Fellowship Baptist of Canada and is still active in pulpit supply.

Tribute to Irene Humphries

I struggled with the idea of what paying tribute to Irene meant and what I, having only known her during illness, could possibly say. However, I jumped at the chance simply because it would afford me the opportunity of searching my own "inner being" and possibly gain a better understanding of our own limitations in terms of achieving symptom control for our patients and ultimately, a peaceful death.

Irene's suffering was profound and the suffering of her husband and family right along side. Her desire to remain at home was not realized due in large part to lack of pain control and along with that, a lack of trust and confidence in being able to manage her care at home. Through it all, Irene was always hopeful and whenever a new plan was devised, her statement was always "well I hope it will work now".

Irene took time to prepare for death (it was Jim who told me, not her). She wrote, prayed and set up special times with her children, grandchildren and friends. She didn't blame her circumstances but at times must have found disappointment and fear overwhelming because of the sheer responsibility of living with pain and dealing with changes in body image, etc. Often when I visited, her Bible, prayer book and journal were right beside her. My reasons for visiting were sometimes selfish because I wanted to know more about how people actually do this thing called "living while dying". Irene was a person who probably had more questions than answers and would often challenge our preconceived ideas about how this gets lived out. Irene's deep desire was to do this right and often in the living of each moment she could transcend the darkness of separation and still enjoy life. She didn't explain the process, but simply lived it: she planned renovations to their home (which were completed), she gardened, planted flowers and tended them, and she planned special trips with children and grandchildren. These times together were rich and meaningful but always there was the realization of parting – both joy and sorrow were present at each event.

I will always remember Irene, who blessed and enriched my life, and taught me a valuable lesson, namely that of humility. The final journey is unique to each person (it's their own) and what a privilege it is to be allowed to share in that most sacred space.

Thank you Irene!

Anne Plett - Head Palliative Care Nurse for South-Eastern Manitoba. A true angel of mercy, who walked almost daily with Jim and Irene for two and a half years.

The dictionary defines a servant as a person working in the service of another. Grace is likened unto a state of sanctification by God; the state of one whom is under such divine influence. If this is indeed the meaning belonging to these words, Irene would have been an example of both. She was indeed working for the service for, and sanctified by, God.

I recently read a book that talked about what is called "tipping points" in our society. Times when a fashion craze just takes off or crime just seemingly all of a sudden drops. What happens to bring this about? The book went on to mention three different types of people who are instrumental in bringing about these changes. One of them was called "connectors". They are people, when you meet them, whom you are instantly drawn to and trust with almost certainty right away. I look at the characteristics of a connector – people who love to engage others no matter where they are, people whom others feel an immediate trust to, people who simply put, love other people.

I look at this and can't help but recognize that "connector personality" in Irene. If you ever had a chance to sit and talk with her, you would immediately notice that she loved to engage people in conversation. Chatting with her had the characteristic of "home", a safe place, and a soft place to land. Come to think of it – combining the characteristics of connector would be pretty close to the definition of servant.

At a ladies retreat one year, I had the privilege to sit in on Irene's testimony. If you haven't heard it, all I can say is – wow! I can't imagine what my life might look like if I had been placed in the circumstances that she experienced. Her life story is definitely one of grace. She was under His influence, sanctified by Him.

But I say this because I feel that although she had received His grace for troubles she had encountered, it seems to me that God's graciousness through the times of turmoil with her children were of precious measure to her. If you take out work from her life, you would still have Irene. If you take out travel and ministry from her life, you would even still have Irene. But if you took out her husband, her children and her grandchildren, Irene would not be Irene anymore. She not only received grace to deal with the difficulties of raising children, but poured out grace to them as well. Never was there a time when you would talk to her that she would not speak about her family.

Irene was, as I mentioned, a "connector". A connector (used as a servant, a model of grace) did just that – connected people. They are a rare variety that God uses to create change in other people's lives and in the world that they live around. I think that would summarize Irene's life – a servant of grace used by God to connect people to her Lord and to each other.

Dominique Kozarchuk - Former Office Administrator of Project L.A.M.B.S. International Inc. Now working for Youth For Christ, as a "Host" at Camp Cedarwood.

Curtis Krahn, M.D., C.C.F.P.*

STEINBACH FAMILY MEDICAL CENTER
333 LOEWEN BLVD BOX 849 STEINBACH MB R5G 1A2
PHONE (204) 326-8852 FAX (204) 326-3899
www.steinbachfamilymedical.com

Dr. Jesus Christ
Great Physician Encounters
777 Celestial Blvd

RE: IRENE HUMPHRIES
DOB: March 20, 1950

Dear Jesus;

Sorry to bother you with this request, but we have been unsuccessful with our treat-to-cure intent and are asking for you to take over Irene's care. I believe you know Irene from your previous long therapeutic relationship with her.

We have previously dealt surgically and chemotherapeutically with her issues but feel we need your expert help in this case. In fact, she is taking you up on your offer to accept without hesitation all those patients who request transfer. She has apparently read your mission statement and has really bought into the whole relationship paradigm, as I have.

Irene has always been very easy to work with. She is always compliant with treatment, (which should work out well as we understand that your yoke is easy and your burden light). In reality I hate to see her go as she has been one of my easier patients to deal with. Sometimes the doctor-patient relationship becomes one of the patient benefiting the doctor more that the doctor benefits the patient. But why am I telling you this? You know more about relationships than I do.

Thanks again for accepting her into Your care.

Sincerely,

Curtis Krahn. M.D.. C.C.F.P.*

Dr. Krahn - Steinbach Cancer Care Unit, Physician and a gifted man in serving and walking with the sick and needy.

One of the most commonly asked questions is why do good people suffer so much; especially those that are believers in the Lord Jesus Christ.

As we search the Scriptures, it is very clear that there are many answers to this question.

Suffering for believers in Christ comes in different forms, and for different reasons. In the book of Job, we read that Satan asked God for permission to challenge Job's love for God, by taking Job's wealth and bringing great sickness upon Job's body. But Job proved himself faithful to the end.

James wrote in James 5:10 "Take my brethren, the prophets who have spoken in the name of the Lord, for an example of sufferings, afflictions, and patience. Behold we count them happy which endure. Ye have heard of the patience of Job, and have seen the end of the Lord; that the Lord is pitiful, and of tender mercy".

In Luke 22:31, the Lord Jesus said to Peter, "Simon, Simon, behold Satan hath desired to have you, that I may sift you as wheat. But I have prayed for you that thy faith fail not". We learn that the accuser of the brethren (Satan) is constantly accusing us before the Lord in order to test us and destroy us. We also learn that sometimes God allows him to test us while He is depending on us to stand firm in our faith in Him, and that our faith faint not. Paul tells us in II Corinthians 9, of the thorn in his flesh. He said that it was given to him to keep him humble. He sought the Lord three times for deliverance and the Lord told him that His grace was sufficient to keep him. We also see in Acts 9:15, Paul was called to be a chosen vessel unto the Lord to bear His name before the Gentiles and to suffer great things for the name of the Lord. John 9, records the story of a man that was suffering from blindness from birth. The disciples asked Jesus, "Who did sin, this man or his parents, why he was born blind?" Jesus answered, "He was born blind that the works of God should be made manifest in him".

None of us knows about tomorrow, or next month or next year, whether or not we will be called upon to suffer for the Lord Jesus, so that His glory should manifest in us to bring glory to His name and be a witness to someone here on this earth. We do know from I Peter 2:21, "For even hereunto were we called, because Christ also suffered for us, leaving us an example that we should follow His steps". We know from Philippians 1:29, "For unto you it is given in the behalf of Christ not only to believe on Him, but also to suffer for His sake". We are encouraged in I Peter 4:19, "Wherefore let him that suffers according to the will of God commit the keeping of their souls to Him in well doing as unto a faithful creator".

When suffering comes to the believer in Christ, whether by persecution or by sickness, I believe it comes from the enemy of our souls (Satan) who goes around as a roaring lion seeking who he can devour that he may destroy their faith in the Lord Jesus. Sometimes the Lord allows us to go through fiery trials which to try us as though some strange things have happened to us.

The late Rev. Irene Humphries was one of the godliest women I have ever met. She was a humble servant to the Lord; reflecting the beauty of Jesus Christ with love and compassion. Yet we saw her suffer with cancer and then she was taken from us to her eternal reward. We saw her suffer as a champion. We never saw her wavering in her faith in Christ; not being bitter and not asking why me? She always knew that the final word about her situation was in the hands of her Lord. She also knew that if she suffered in His will, she would also reign with Him.

We at the West Indian Christian Fellowship learned from our beloved sister, the late Rev. Irene Humphries that God is God. In good or bad times, on the mountaintop or down in the valley; God is still God. In sickness or in health; God is God. In life or in death; God is still God.

Who shall separate us from the love of God in Christ Jesus; shall tribulations or distress or persecution or peril? As it is written for Thy sake we are killed all the day long; we are accounted as sheep for the slaughter. Nay in all these things we are more than conquerors through Him For I am persuaded that neither death, nor life, nor angels, nor principalities nor powers nor things to come nor height, nor depth nor any other creatures shall separate us from the love of God which is in Christ Jesus our Lord. To God be the glory! Amen.

David Rose - Jamaican Pastor and close friend from Winnipeg, Manitoba.

Irene Humphries was a most refreshing and wonderful Christian woman, who lived without prejudice. She was the loving and faithful wife of Jim for the past 32 years, the mother of Joshua and Rachel, and the grandmother of Adrienna, Jeremy, Sadie, Tyah and Anna-Irene. Her last granddaughter was born the day before her passing, and is now her namesake.

Irene's passion for Jesus Christ was shown in her service with the Christian Mission, "The Voice of the Martyrs" during her teen years. Following marriage, Irene and Jim were committed to active service to God throughout their lives together. In 2001 Irene completed her Master's degree with Providence Seminary, and was formally ordained as a Christian minister in 2000. Irene's teaching ministry was poignant, relevant, and engaging.

Following a severe bout with cancer, God gave Irene an eighteen-month reprieve wherein she and Jim were able to resume their Mobile Bible College ministry. Many of us celebrated Irene's recovery and her visits to our communities. We were so blessed by Irene's presence at our Canadian convention last fall in Winnipeg. She was radiant! Her physical revival and reprieve afforded her, a final trip to Jamaica wherein Irene was honoured by her loyal and loving Jamaican brothers and sisters.

Irene was a rock of godly stability and a consistently good person. She was always approachable, sincere, and encouraging. Irene will be greatly missed by Jim, her family, and by all of us, - her friends. "We love you Irene, - and we thank God for giving you to us all." We share our heart-felt condolences with Jim, Joshua, Rachel and their families. We look forward to meeting Irene – "in the morning".

Pastor Glen Forsberg - Long time co-worker, friend and mentor to Jim and Irene – Now Senior Pastor of McMurray Gospel Church in Alberta.

My memory of Irene Humphries is a very vivid one. I saw her suffer beyond words and yet she always found a way to praise and bless the Lord. She would thank the Lord for all she had, no matter what she was going through.

My journey with Irene started one night at 11 pm about four years before her cancer returned. Jim phoned me and asked if I could come and sit with Irene because she was in a lot of pain and the doctor could not find what was wrong with her. She had had quite a lot of pain for a few days already, but finally at 4 am the pain started to subside enough so she could finally fall asleep. As I went home, I already realized how much she depended on the Lord to help her bear the pain and how He would help her through all her trials. As she prayed throughout this ordeal, she would praise the Lord and thank Him for blessing her with the doctors and nurses. She was always considerate of the time they were devoting to her care. She used to think she was taking too much of their time.

Then we would see each other on an occasional basis. Our friendship was quite unique. Jim and Irene were working on Project L.A.M.B.S. and they were very busy getting it started. She seemed to be quite healthy. I volunteered with them for a few years during the time my daughter Wendy was helping type the curriculum. They flew all over the world with Project L.A.M.B.S.; places I would not dream of visiting. She was having a great time visiting different parts of the world and co-teaching with Jim.

Then in 2002, Irene was having a lot of pain again and this time the news she got was not very good. I knew that I would be involved in her care. The Holy Spirit had already prepared my heart for this time. I drove onto the hospital parking lot once and drove right off again. I knew in my heart what was waiting when I entered those doors. Then I did go in and she gave me the bad news. The bad news was that her cancer was back and they did not think they could treat it. She asked me if I would help her as she walked this part of her journey. I agreed to look after her as best I could.

I helped her with many different needs. I would sit with her, hold her hand and tried in my meagre way to comfort her. She had a lot of pain most of the time she battled cancer. She taught me much about the love of God the next few years. She braved her cancer treatment. Her cancer went into remission and the Lord granted her a few more years in answer to her prayers. She requested some more time that she could better prepare her children for the time when she would need to leave her earthly home for her eternal home in Heaven. She wanted to pray a blessing on each of her children and grandchildren. She wanted them to know where she was going and that it was her wish that they all would meet again in Heaven. She always prayed that she would not vomit during her chemo treatment and He graciously granted her that answer to her request as well. She was very grateful for that.

Irene and I had some wonderful times together, praying, sharing, as well as shopping. We had a great time when we went shopping for her wig. One day she asked me to cut her hair because they were starting to fall out. John and I took a day off to go shopping with Jim and Irene. I don't remember what John and Jim did, but Irene and I went looking for just the right hairpiece. She remarked that she would gladly wear the hairpiece as long as she did not have to vomit.

Jim and Irene were planning to respond to a request that they come to Myanmar to teach their Bible School. She had an oncology appointment the day before they were to leave. Her blood count was good and all signs were there that she was still in remission. She felt fine, so they left for Myanmar. Once they arrived in Myanmar, she developed a pain in her back. They thought that it was as a result of the long flight and the long times she had to stand while teaching. She went for several massages, took painkillers, but her pain would only dull, not subside.

When Jim and Irene returned home, there was a message on their answering machine to call their doctor as soon as possible. One of the blood tests they had taken came back a few days after they left. It revealed that her cancer was back. They told her that this time there was not much they could do for her because if they treated this cancer, it would have to be done very aggressively and with the kind of cancer she had, she would likely get another one on the heels of this one going away. So they decided that no treatment would be done. They would simply try to keep her comfortable. I was in Toronto with John when Irene called me to tell me her devastating news. She asked me to come over to discuss her care as soon as I got home. When I returned home, I went to visit her. We talked about what was to come and how she wanted me to look after her. What a privilege it was to talk with Irene about her going home to be with Jesus. In Irene's case, however, it was the Lord's chariot coming for her. She was so much looking forward to going to be with Jesus, but so much she longed to remain with her family. She realized that was not to be, so she tried her best to deal with it.

She was a very private person and therefore tried very hard to restrict her company. She did not want to display her suffering to everyone. She worked hard at keeping the pain under control and she did not always have answers to all the questions people would ask her.

One thing that sticks out in my mind was when her children would come to visit. She could have been fighting the pain, but she would try hard to suppress it. It reminded me of a certain flower that opens up and reaches for the sky. She would open up and worked hard at staying open as long as they were there. When they would leave, she would deal with the pain. It was as though God would grant her good times with her family. Controlling her pain proved to be impossible. Her pain was just too intense. It was a long few months for Irene. She could hardly stand the pain at times. So many times she would say, "Jesus, Jesus, help me!"

I have many painful memories of Irene. She had so much pain; so much too much pain. But Irene would not want to be remembered for the pain she endured. She said that Jesus suffered so much more and she was looking expectantly forward to going and being with her Lord and Saviour. She was waiting for the Lord to send a chariot for her. He had shown her or Jim a picture of this chariot. She talked about the people that were waiting in heaven for her to arrive. Some of the people she talked about were her mother and my son Randy. He always was so fond of Jim and Irene. He would have loved to work with them in Project L.A.M.B.S.

John and I spent a lot of time with Jim and Irene the last few months of her life. I never thought that I would be by her side when she passed into eternity. I considered it an honour to be there when her chariot came for her. The last weeks of her life, Irene spent in the Palliative Care ward at St. Boniface Hospital. It is hard to imagine how much she depended on the Lord to help her. She was so much looking forward to the end of her suffering, which would mean she would spend eternity in Heaven with Jesus. Through all the pain, she remained steadfast in her faith in God. She continually prayed blessings on the staff and the people that were taking care of her. These people fell in love with Irene. All the staff were cheering her on and looking forward together with her for the coming of her new grandchild. When her granddaughter was born, they all rejoiced with her. She was so excited. She saw the baby pictures and Jim assured her that all was well. He encouraged her that she could now go and be with Jesus, and she did.

Mathilda Fehr - Close friend and caregiver to Irene. Dedicated to walking with Irene 24/7. The only one who was with me at the moment of Irene's home-going.

TRIBUTE TO IRENE

My earliest memory of Irene was in youth at Full Gospel Chapel, where Jimmer and Irene were pastoring. I was a new Christian and I felt somewhat out of place in the church environment. I will never forget the sincerity of Irene's greetings, when she asked, "How are you?" She really wanted to know.

Being a new Christian I would observe very closely the behaviour of the Christians around me. I was immediately drawn to Irene's spirit; she had such a gentle spirit and such compassion and most importantly, a genuine heart for God. I would watch her in amazement, thinking she can't be like this all the time. She was though, this was her genuine self. I felt like a bull in a china shop around her, yet she treated me with value and importance.

Jimmer and Irene fostered teenage children as well. I became friends with one of their foster daughters, which allowed me to spend a lot of time in their home. You could feel the love when you walked through the doors of their house. Irene was always making sure there were snacks and that everyone was comfortable and happy. If Linda would want to do something or go somewhere she was not allowed; Irene would calmly explain why she and Jimmer were saying "No".

Irene was such a devoted wife and mother, instilling godly values into Josh and Rachel and any foster children in their care. Living out what they preached in church and youth. She was so supportive of Jimmer. I marvelled at their union. She was so submissive and yet not a doormat, she had such dignity and stature as she walked alongside her husband; a true testimony of commitment.

One thing that Irene said to me one day last year will stick with me forever. We were talking on the street and I asked her if she was scared (in regards to the cancer and death). Her response was this, "I am going to die living, not live dying." What an attitude, it changes your whole perspective. I can only pray I have the same courage if I ever have to go through such trials. There is a large void in the community since Irene's passing, but heaven has gained the sweetest angel.

In closing, I would like to share a picture I had the privilege of seeing. On the day of Irene's funeral, when they were rolling out her casket, the song, "I Can Only Imagine" was playing. I closed my eyes and began to cry. My thoughts were, "why God, she was doing so much for you here?" At that point in the song the lyrics said, "Will I dance before you Jesus or in awe of You be still". I saw Irene, her beautiful, radiant, restored self. Her arms were raised in worship to her King and she was dancing on streets of gold. My question went from why to why not. Although she is greatly, greatly missed here, she is now seated in the heavenlies and I have a feeling she is enjoying it there.

This portion of scripture has always reminded me of Irene, I will share just a few of the key verses from Proverbs 31:10-31.

Prov. 31:10-12: *A wife of noble character who can find? She is worth far more than rubies. Her husband has full confidence in her and lacks nothing of value. She brings him good; not harm, all the days of her life.*

Prov. 3:20: *She opens her arms to the poor and extends her hands to the needy.*

Prov. 31:23: *Her husband is respected at the city gate, where he takes his seat among the elders of the land.*

Prov. 31:25-31: *She is clothed with strength and dignity; she can laugh at the days to come. She speaks with wisdom, and faithful instruction is on her tongue. She watches over the affairs of her household and does not eat the bread of idleness. Her children arise and call her blessed; her husband also, and he praises her. "Many women do noble things, but you surpass them all." Charm is deceptive and beauty fleeting; but a woman who fears the Lord is to be praised. Give her the reward she has earned, and let her works bring her praise at the city gate.*

You are missed my friend!
Love, Karen Friesen

Karen Friesen - Friend, supporter and board member of Project L.A.M.B.S. International Inc. Co-owner of Imperial Metals, Steinbach, MB.

How do I put into words what someone like Irene means to me? She was a teacher, a friend, an example of a godly woman. She inspired me to believe that God could use even me in ministry.

She was an inspiring teacher! When I attended Project L.A.M.B.S. courses, she was so excited to show us what God had shown her, that her enthusiasm was infectious! When she would teach on a particular subject, she would be so thorough, she would challenge me to search deeper on my own. She had a way of bringing the Word to life!

She was a worshipper! The last time I saw her, she was attending a Women's Christmas event, where I was leading the worship. It was evident that her physical body was struggling, but when she closed her eyes, and lifted her hands to heaven, I knew she was worshipping a God that she knew intimately, who was expecting her arrival in heaven soon.

She encouraged me to reach for everything God had for me as a woman. She was always beautifully dressed, always radiant, a real example of a gracious, classy lady.

I feel privileged and blessed for having had the opportunity to have known and loved her.

Bev Loewen - Long time fellow worshipper and friend of Irene's. Wife of Peter Loewen of Eastern Nissan, Steinbach, MB.

My Reflections of Irene

So much comes to my mind as I sit here reflecting on Irene. As one of my Mom's dearest friends, I was often included and enjoyed special "girl times" with Irene, whether she was getting together for tea or going out for lunch with ladies. She made me feel like a friend too, and not just her friend's daughter. I noticed that she always showed an interest in anyone she spoke to. She always wanted to know how you were doing and what you were busy with. She had a way about her that just made you feel so special. She always made me feel that way. Even in her final months, struggling with pain, she'd ask me how I was and showed an interest in my life that blew me away. Never have I seen such a selfless, strong and sweet spirit. She leaves an unforgettable impression upon my heart that I will carry with me always.

I had the privilege of attending a Ladies Retreat several years back with Irene as the main speaker. The theme of the retreat was "Growing in Grace". How she loved to speak of God's grace and minister to others. I'll also never forget the classes I attended where she taught on Romans. She was excited to teach it and I can still hear her voice as she passionately taught on the grace and righteousness of God. It was so alive to her and God used her to bring the Scriptures alive for each of us as well. She taught from the heart. It was clearly evident that God had made these Scriptures very real to her; very dear to her own heart. It caused her teaching to be incredibly effective. She would share from her life experiences as she taught, making her so real and down to earth as well.

Irene was a princess. She had such a beautiful sense of style, not only in her appearance but in her home decorating. (We shared a love of home decorating shows!) But aside from all that it was her beautiful spirit that made her a true princess, a daughter of the King.

Her love for her husband spoke to my heart. How she honoured Jim on his 50th birthday! As we decorated together for the event, she was so excited to do this for him and wanted it to be very special. She wanted her "manservant" to feel like "king for a day". Whenever she referred to Jim as her "manservant", it was always with such love. It was never demeaning in the least. She was so grateful for all he did to care for her. She always expressed such love for her children and grandchildren as well.

It doesn't seem like very long ago we were decorating for the Project LA.M.B.S. Christmas Banquet. What a party that was...such a joyful atmosphere! I'm so glad she lived to see that big crowd of beautiful faces who'd all come in support of her and Pastor Jim and their ministry. She touched each and every heart that night with her powerful message.

It's still with great emotion that I remember the last time I saw Irene. My Mom and I and our friend Karen went to have tea with her one morning. This was just a few days before she went into the hospital. She was in great pain and it was very difficult to see her like that. We had all brought Scriptures to share with her and we gathered around and prayed for her. Yet, despite the excruciating morning she'd had, she also wanted to pray for us. Her selfless prayers for us meant more than any words here can express. No matter what she was going through she ministered to others. I thought it was so fitting at her funeral when fellow ministers lined up on either side of the aisle to honour her as the casket left the church.

I loved Irene and am so honoured to be able to pay tribute to her memory in this small way.

Irene, I can only imagine what you are all experiencing now in God's glorious presence. How incredible it all must be. I can picture you in my mind, worshipping God in a field of daisies. Until we meet again..."embrace your reward, fair princess".

Sheila Delaurier – a little friend with a big heart of prayer for Irene and her ministry. From LaBroquerie, Manitoba

Irene's friendship was a gift from God – for a time – for a season on this earth – but to be continued on forever in heaven. As a Child of God she kissed death goodbye, changed flights and went home forever; never to be sick, never to be sad, and never to be afraid again.

She was a spirit of gentleness, peace and love. She fought the good fight, she ran the race, when she fell she got back up and continued on until the finish. The night before she left us, we held hands and prayed. She could not speak but we knew she was there, as her body became peaceful from a very restless state.

I thought of Jesus as He prayed to His heavenly Father. "If it is possible, please take this cup from me" and "I commit My Spirit into Thy hands." What a battle! I watched Irene in the valley of death. I watched her sing, play, cry, and obediently give herself to God, as she struggled with her body. She hung on to God for all she was worth. Trusting God to come and rescue her, and He did.

She was real; she was courageous, and she was a light for Jesus. We miss her and look forward to forever in heaven – to laugh again.

Thank you IRENE for the time we had together.

Love, Myrna

Myrna Penner – Another angel of mercy who especially blessed Irene with much love, compassion and tears. In humbleness of spirit, she blessed Irene by massaging and washing her feet with tears, to show her deep love for Irene and her ministry. Many times she would hold Irene in her arms to comfort her.

Tribute to Rev. Irene Humphries

I have many fond recollections and lasting memories of our dear sister Irene Humphries. There are a few however, that stand out as specific highlights worth mentioning in this tribute.

It was an awesome privilege for me to participate in the ordination ceremony of Rev. Irene, representing the Fellowship of Christian Assemblies. She looked absolutely radiant and spoke eloquently as she was ordained for ministry, which was an honour well deserved.

Another special memory was on the occasion of Shalom's 10th Anniversary Thanksgiving Banquet in October of 2003. Our guest speaker had to cancel due to an emergency and I prayed as to who would be a suitable replacement at very short notice. Sister Irene came to mind and she willingly accepted and shared her testimony of God's grace in the midst of severe personal trials. At that point she had indeed experienced a healing and a reprieve from the cancer and she gave glory to God. There wasn't a dry eye in the house and all of the banquet guests were impressed by her dignity and humility and her faith that was her victory.

Pastor Dave Reimer - Long time friend and area minister of the Fellowship of Christian Assemblies of Manitoba.

My relationship and friendship go back to the time Jim and Irene, Joshua and Rachel moved to Steinbach, in the early 80's. Within a short period of time we realized we had some similar giftings – Irene and I spent many hours creating, I must say, some magnificent pieces of construction paper artwork for the Travelodge in Winnipeg.

As a young Christian at that time and eager to go into the ministry, Irene prayed with me many times on our drive to and from Winnipeg.

Our respective ministries took us to a number of different places, but our friendship always resumed from where it left off throughout the years, as our paths again crossed.

Irene was an example of faith, always pursuing God; realizing the more we know, the more we know we don't know, and want to know Him more.

Pastor Katie Reimer – Long time friend and worked together with Irene in the Fellowship of Christian Assemblies in Steinbach.

The treasure of friendship in this earthen vessel

Tucked away in the corner of my heart are treasured memories of one godly woman—Irene Humphries. She was a tiny, quietly dynamic teacher of the Word of God, a lover of Jesus. She opened up the Word and made it alive and exciting. She was an inspiration to me and to many others.

She was a good example of a virtuous woman—a wonderful helpmeet to Pastor Jim and a caring, loving Mom and Grandmother to her children and grandchildren. Their actions and accomplishments were touted each time we spoke on the phone.

Her ministry has not gone unnoticed in the Kingdom of God and His people. Her love in action, like ripples from a pebble dropped in a pond will have reached further and accomplished more than we will ever know and appreciate in this short life!

I treasure the memories of our times together—hiking the trails (and getting lost) around Fort McMurray, the picking of clover for tea (who knew there'd be so many bugs hiding in it!) and admiring and appreciating God's beautiful world. The times we enjoyed together were not quite enough!

I treasure the newsletters mailed during her last earthly months attesting to the goodness of Jesus in her life. How like her—to honour Christ's faithfulness to the very end. I was in awe and challenged while reading them.

The treasure of our friendship will carry on when we meet in heaven. When I see her again she will have on a crown of life given to those who endure, who are over comers of adversity, who are faithful to the end.

Irene was a blessing to many and the memory of her friendship is a valued treasure of mine.

Carole Argo – Former secretary at McMurray Gospel Fellowship and special friend and encourager to Irene and Jim. Now living in Edmonton, AB

YOU ARE MINE

1. I will come to you in the silence,
I will lift you from all your fear.
You will hear my voice,
I claim you as my choice,
Be still and know I am here.

2. I am hope for all who are hopeless.
I am eyes for all who long to see.
In the shadows of the night,
I will be your light,
Come and rest in me.

REFRAIN:
Do not be afraid, I am with you.
I have called you each by name.
Come and follow me,
I will bring you home;
I love you and you are mine.

3. I am strength for all the despairing,
Healing for the ones who dwell in shame.
All the blind will see,
The lame will all run free,
And all will know my name.

4. I am the Word that leads all to freedom,
I am the peace the world cannot give.
I will call your name,
Embracing all your pain,
Stand up, now walk, and live.

Brigitte Remillard – A caregiver, servant and nurse from St. Boniface Palliative Care Unit in Winnipeg. She sang this song to Irene just a few days before her home going.

As I sat in the pew and opened Irene's obituary, the words on the page seemed to hit me straight in the heart. I had lost a few loved ones before, but I had never read of a life like this. A paragraph rich with the achievements of a woman who devoted her entire life to the God she loved.

I shared a friendship with Irene during the beginning of her latest and dearest ministry, Project L.A.M.B.S. She was 47, and I was 19. We were both embarking upon new seasons in our lives. A time filled with anticipation, excitement and adventure. Over a mug of hot coffee or car ride into town, she would share fascinating stories of when she was my age. She said I reminded her of herself when she was young. Although it was something said casually, the words remained imprinted deep within me. She was an accomplished and talented woman and that I greatly admired. She was sincere, kind, and she carried a peace so enveloping it could calm a storm in your soul just by being near her.

One afternoon shortly before her passing, I asked for her opinion. "Should I go back to art school?" "How long is the program?" she asked. "Three years", I answered. She looked off and replied, "Yeah, I'd do that. Three years is nothing." (Jim playfully reminded her she already had a master's degree, and wasn't that enough?) Her laid back response struck me immediately. This reply coming from a woman that admits she's packed five lifetimes into 54 years. Once again, I left with her simple words stamped in my mind.

I've kept a copy of Irene's obituary. It's less than 200 words and more moving than any book I've found. Rereading it seems to be a constant source of empowerment for me. Amazingly, she has inspired me more since her passing. When I see all of her accomplishments, and her life of servant-hood jam-packed into one small paragraph, it makes me wish that mine could look the same. And knowing she saw a little of herself in me makes me believe it can.

"Give her the reward she has earned, and let her works bring her praise at the city gate."

-- Proverbs 31:31

Gloria Klassen - Former secretary of Project L.A.M.B.S. International Inc., and long time friend and artist.

I'm No Ordinary Person

I'm no ordinary person
I am a true pearl
Skilfully created in a mould made just for me.

I am a virtuous woman
You can't buy me
My price is far above rubies
And my worth greater than gold
Even fine gold

I'm no ordinary mother
I bore my young in great pain
And knew immediately
That by the sweat of my brow
They must eat bread

You see, I'm industrious
I am ambitious
I am bold
I am beautiful
I am proud
I'm just not ordinary

I'm a lover, I'm strong
I am courageous!
I'm a sojourner not a dweller
I am a survivor
I am Mrs. Irene Humphries
And remember I'm no ordinary person.

Written by: Karen Hamilton-Reid – Student, teacher and special friend from Jamaica to Irene. Irene attended Karen's wedding in Jamaica just weeks before her home going.

Words are not sufficient to express how we feel at this moment. We sit and reminisce about the time you spent with us. It was Easter of 1997 when we first met Pastor and Sis Humphries. They were guest speakers at our annual convention. Little did we know that this was the first of many meetings to come? Approximately one year after this they took up the great challenge of teaching Bible School in our fellowship. Project L.A.M.B.S., it was called. It seemed ironic for the school to be called LAMBS when we were quite aware that some of our attitudes were goat like. Discipleship was the base of the school.

Pastor and Sis Humphries were very patient and understanding with us as they poured out of their hearts and souls the passion they had for God. We were not always easy to deal with but their loving and understanding mannerisms tempered the situations that arose. Sis Irene was a woman of class. It was obvious in her dress, her speech and the manner in which she attended to each of us. Behind every successful man, they say, is a good woman. Good is just one of the many descriptive words that can be used to outline the characteristics of Sis Humphries.

We recall the teaching of the book of Romans – "Romans-Road to Salvation". She taught us a portion of that series of lessons and all sat in awe and listened attentively. She made us laugh in class; she made us cry, she commanded our attention in her sweet and gentle way. We felt the Spirit of God flow from her to us when she laid her hands on us in prayer. We felt the love that emanated from her heart when she held us in her arms.

Sis Irene was ordained as Pastor, right here in Jamaica with our own. She honoured her role and actively carried out her pastoral duties efficiently and effectively under the leading of God's anointing.

Today we pay tribute to a woman of noble character, a mother, a sister and a friend. Words aren't sufficient to express our feelings towards our Pastor. Pastor Irene is one of us, a true example of a genuine Christian.

We salute her and esteem her highly. Pastor Irene Humphries, you have melted our hearts, moulded our lives and created footprints across the sand of our hearts that will never be washed away. You have reached the depth of our souls through your commitment. Even in your greatest need you still gave unselfishly to us. We miss you, we love you, and we will never forget you. We will meet you some glad day around God's throne. We love you. See you soon.

Love Always,
The Family of the Independent Assemblies of God of Jamaica

A Beracah Person

The word Beracah came from 2 Chronicles 20. As Jehosaphat went through a time of war in his life and his kingdom, and did not know what to do, he turned to the Lord for help, and God answered him through another priest who had a gift of prophecy. Although five kings came against Jehosaphat, God encouraged him not to be afraid. Ultimately, God gave Jehosaphat victory. The promise of God came through. The enemies of Jehosaphat were defeated, and the children of God took home their spoils of war. The Valley where the people of God praised Him was called Beracah, "The Valley of Praise".

As I think of what to say about my dear sister, friend and mother in the Lord, I cannot but call her "BERACHA". She was blessed and she was a blessing. When we met, little did I know that both of us would enter into a unique relationship like we had. Irene was a gift to me. She was my inspiration. She was my encourager, my quiet model of wisdom and incredible wisdom. I feel I am at a loss for the appropriate words to describe her. She let me into her life as if we grew up together. There was no hidden agenda both in her public and private life. She was plain, gentle and straight forward, and she impacted me that way, and charged me to continue the way I have been because it was our gift of transparency that brought us together in the first place, through the power of God.

During the last few days of her life, I went to visit her. Irene did something that only my earthly father (an ordained minister of blessed memory) did when I was called into the ministry. Before I accepted public position in the ministry, my father called me forward to lay his hands on me and prayed for me as Paul did with Timothy. On Irene's deathbed, she whispered to me to come close, and asked me to hold her hand and give her a hug. As we held each other crying, she began to bless me and prophesy over me from the depth of her spirit. She seemed to have transferred her spiritual gifts "unto" me that day (if there is anything like that). We were both there as long as we both felt comfortable not minding those who were there with us. By the time we let go of each other, we were both ready to release one another into the hands of the living God. She died two days later. I am so thankful that I did not miss that opportunity of a lifetime.

On the day of her burial, I was given a "mantle" at such a time that I was going through some processing moments in my ministry life. The message that came with the gift of that mantle confirmed to me that I am in the right place doing the right thing at the right time. So, I stayed put. Now that she is gone, I continue to think of her as one of the "cloud of witnesses in the sky" cheering me on. I named her "Daughter of Encouragement". I do not think I will run out of words when the opportunity comes to talk to Irene. For now, I can only say, "good night and sleep well". You have given me so much, and I cherish it in this life. I pray that I will be able to make an indelible impact on those I come across here on earth. That is, one that will also have an eternal impact after this life. You are indeed a blessing.

With the love of Christ we shared, I remain your sister and daughter in the faith.

Deborah Olukoju – Fellow labourer in the Lord from Nigeria. One of the Leaders of the Princesses of the Kingdom that Irene was a speaker for and part of.

Tribute in Memory of Irene Humphries

Our hearts are saddened by the passing on of our sister and mother Irene Humphries. My wife and I came to know Jim and Irene barely two years ago, and those two years have been the richest of our eighteen years of ministry. Irene showed us a perfect example of the love Jesus has for us all, and the compassion and forgiveness and suffering with courage and humility, she was an example of commitment and perseverance in the midst of suffering and pain.

During the last days of Irene's life, we were privileged to visit with her. Even though our intention for the visit was to encourage her, we left rather being encouraged and anointed to be more dedicated to our calling. One of her last words to us was to remain committed to our walk with the Lord and the work He has called us to. She reminded us that, the Lord has a purpose for our lives in Canada and we should not lose that.

Irene, we miss you and cannot wait to see you again in glory with the risen Lord.

Rev. Joseph and Grace Seidu – A special family from Ghana who now Pastor the Crestview Park Free Methodist Church in Winnipeg. He also oversees our African Ministry at Project L.A.M.B.S. International Inc. office.

World Wide Tributes & Reflections
- Kachin Connection, Yangon, Myanmar

We are deeply touched at the life and passing of our dear friend and sister in Christ, Irene. Our memories of Irene surely are pleasant ones. What struck me most was her sincerity and humility. She was the kind of person who the Lord enjoys using mightily. She was always willing to serve others sacrificially without reward and her commitment to those she served was of the highest standard.

Irene was one of the greatest supporters of our "Kachin Connection" ministry and I'll never forget how proud she looked when she showed up at one of our support banquets in Winnipeg wearing the Kachin "longyi" (similar to the Indian sarong) she had purchased at one of our craft sales. She wore it so proudly – until I told her it was a man's garment! She blushed, grinned widely and both of us had a good laugh!

In February of 2004 we had the pleasure of hosting Jim and Irene in Myanmar as they presided over the graduation ceremony for the very first L.A.M.B.S. graduation there. Irene was the delight of the school! The students will always remember her genuine interest and encouragement in the minutest details of their lives. She was also deeply touched and concerned over the welfare of the people in this troubled country and over the wellbeing of our missionary family. Her genuine interest and faith was a comfort since we always knew that we could count on her prayers no matter what. We will all miss her greatly.

Steve Solomon – Special Missionary and friend to Irene in Myanmar. Director of Project L.A.M.B.S. International Inc. in

Myanmar. The back cover picture came from Irene speaking at the Myanmar Graduation Ceremonies.

I first remember Irene as an "older than usual" student at Providence, working to finish her degree and working on the L.A.M.B.S. curriculum at the same time. She must have been great at juggling many responsibilities at one time. We had a wonderful time with Jim and Irene at their retreat home, walking through the woods and grassy roads together and talking about almost anything (Steve and my kids in tow). She made us all feel at home and relaxed at the meal we shared together that day.

She seemed ready for adventure … what courage to continue the Jamaica work and step into Myanmar after her first bout with cancer! I was amazed as she took on these challenges with a smile.

I could truly see the light of Life flowing through her, touching all around her. The waiter here in Myanmar (Million Coins Restaurant) always asks about "Irene and Jim" every time we are there. May the seeds of her faithful discipleship grow into a bountiful harvest, giving all glory to God.

The church has lost a great woman and it is only our certainty of her status in heaven through the blood of Christ which comforts us. Her testimony will endure for many years in our hearts and in the telling of her story, which we will continue to share.

"Death is swallowed up in victory.
O death, where is your victory?
O death, where is your sting?"

For sin is the sting that results in death,
and the law gives sin its power.
how we thank God,
who gives us victory over sin and death,
through Jesus Christ our Lord!

I Corinthians 15:54-57

Bev Solomon – A special friend and fellow MASTERS student from Providence and is co-missionary with her husband to Myanmar.

Irene,

We know how much you love Jesus Christ.

We know how much you have a desire to spread the
gospel to the world.
We know how much your love to the Kachin people,
Those who are living in the unreached world.
We know how much you love your husband and want to cooperate
for the Lord with him.
We wanted you to live long and work with Jim
for the L.A.M.B.S. in Myanmar.
We were so encouraged when you visited to Myitkyina, Myanmar.
We believe that you yourself were a miracle.
We praised God and exalted His Name because of you.
We prayed for you every day. However, the days that God had
given to you were ended. What can we do?
Yes we praised God for your service and sacrifice.
Irene we are proud of you. You seeded the gospel seed in
Myanmar. Someday you will see the plants and the fruit.
We see that you are satisfied in Heaven.

Your friend in Christ,

Samson Hkalam
Myitkyina, Kachin State
Myanmar

Samson Hkalam – Co-director of our Myanmar Ministry of Project L.A.M.B.S. International Inc. Graduate of Providence Theological Seminary.

Hello,

I really felt unhappy about Irene. I don't know how to write in a tribute or reflection letter. But I really loved her. We met only one week, however, because of her back pain. I took care her two days in her room. So, we have very friendly. I just write about my feeling and experience with her during that week. I don't know it is suitable or not for a memorial book. You can decide it. If it is possible you also need to check my grammar. Now I'm working in school and everything is not so bad. But I need to speak and write English fluently. So, please always pray for me.

- On 23rd February 2004, I met a lovely sweet lady at Myitkyina Baptist Association office.
- At the break time all the LA.M.B.S.students are usually drinking tea (Hpa-Hka) with one kind of Burmese palm sugar. Some one served her and on her hand she had a cup of tea and a square of palm sugar. She asked me the name of that palm sugar in English. I didn't know that name and I have difficult to explain about that palm sugar. At that night I searched in the dictionary and I found.I have kept firmly in my mind that name "Jaggery".Thank You!
- On 24th & 25th she taught about the Kingdom of God to the L.A.M.B.S. students. Because of the long journey she felt tired and pain but both of the afternoon she didn't lose her face.
- On 26th & 27th she felt back pain and she had massage with a masseur. Both days she took a rest on her bed in the YMCA guesthouse. Both that days we talked about similarity between the Kachin alphabets and the English alphabets, some Kachin usage, showed her family's pictures and explained and shared about her surgery experience.

- On 29th February,2004 that day was a wonderful and extraordinary day for the Kachin people. It was the first graduation day of the L.A.M.B.S. Project in Myanmar. She participated in that service with Jim and Steve and gave certificates and appreciated over seventy students with smiling face.
- After the ceremony she hugs me and said, "We will meet again in Canada". However, when I arrived in Canada I have no opportunity to meet with her.
- Dear Irene, I met you only one week, but you left your kind, tender and sweet heart to me. All of your actions are unforgettable for me.

Your sister in Christ,

With Love, Hkaw Win

Hkaw Win – Irene's friend, servant and interpreter while Irene was in Myanmar teaching. She is also the first recipient of $500.00 Irene Humphries Memorial Fund. She is now being Trained at Providence Theological Seminary and will return to teach in the field of Christian Education in Myanmar.

World Wide Tributes & Reflections - EMAILS

Memorial Tribute For:
The Late Rev Irene Humphries

First of all let me say it was a privilege to be able to attend the wake and funeral service for the **Late Rev Irene Humphries.** As a friend and also to represent MGA, their former pastorate.

Pastor Jim Humphries sends his greetings and his love. Pastor Jim and Irene were the ones that built this sanctuary we are sitting in. They are our former Pastors but were always our friends. **In fact Ralph our Drummer got saved under their ministry; Irene** used to go to their house and minister to him.

Pastor Brad Monstion another former Pastor of MGA also sends his greetings and his love.

The theme of the whole funeral was God's Grace. Before Irene passed away she asked Rev Chuck Nichols to speak at her funeral. When he talked to her, he asked her what do you want me to say and she thought for a moment and then said, **do not speak about Irene, but "speak on the grace of God". Dr Nichols said it is not possible to talk about the "grace of God" without talking about Irene.** "1 Peter 5:10 – But the God of all grace who has called you to His eternal glory in Christ Jesus, when ye have suffered for a little while". Suffering for a little while, but Eternal Glory. Irene is now rejoicing with the angels in eternal glory. No more suffering, no more sickness, no more death; but eternal glory.

There is a song that we sing that says, "What a day that will be--- .Another verse says, "There will be no sorrow there---no sickness, no pain---"

I want to share for a few minutes about The Late Irene Humphries. It was a privilege and honour to know such a woman who shone with the love of God. She was and always will be a blessing to both my wife and I.

* A woman who everything she did and said was to glorify God
* A woman that never once complained about her sickness
* A woman that blessed everyone she came in contact with
* A woman who had the heart of God for service
* A woman that was dedicated to serving God no matter where it was
* A woman that before she passed away called in her children and grandchildren and talked to each one alone, anointed them and prayed for them. This was a woman that was dying in her bed.
* A woman that you would visit to minister to and pray for, but when you left it was you that was ministered to and prayed for.
* A woman who touched everyone she came in contact with. This was evident at her funeral where there were people from Jamaica, Africa and numerous other places.
* A woman that was healed two years earlier, then the cancer came back; still she did not curse God, but glorified Him to the end.

At the viewing, it was not a time to stand around and weep for Irene, but they had a service where "Midnight's Cry" sang songs and four people shared about Irene, including Pastor Brad Monstion. They shared little things, humorous things for the kids to know about their mother. It was not a time to be sad, but to rejoice that there was no more pain and now she was with her Father in Heaven. There were numerous mentions of the plan of salvation. Irene's favourite verse was John 3:16.

The funeral service the next day was the same as the viewing; it was a time of celebration with little mourning. There was an honour guard by all the Pastors and Ministers as Irene was taken from the church. It was a sight to see. She touched many people with her dedication to the work of God.

At the graveside, there were a number of different people involved in prayer, scripture reading and singing. All different people, she had touched. A number of them were Africans who were being trained by Pastor Jim and Irene to go back to their homeland and start churches. They were being trained to be Pastors.

Irene had been healed two years earlier and they have the medical records to prove it, but her healing had little effect on those around or her kids. A number of times we almost lost Irene, but she would tell Jim, 'No, I don't believe it is time yet and she would bounce back'. But this time she told her husband Pastor Jim that this time she was going home. This time through her sickness, their kids came back; they are both in the church and serving God. She got to see this before she went home to Heaven. The day before she died, a new granddaughter was born and named Anna-Irene. Pastor Jim showed Irene some video and the pictures the next day and then took her hand and said, 'it is now time to go home, and within a half an hour after that she went to be with the Lord.

At the graveside, it was unique, that the casket that was used was one you could write on with a sharpie. Each of the family first and then friends had the opportunity to write their last goodbye on the casket. It was neat to see that both her kids wrote a number of things but what stood out was **"I will see you again Mom"**. It was very moving. Then I had the privilege to assist in lowering the casket into the ground.

Pastor Brad and I had the opportunity to spend the night with Pastor Jim at his home after the funeral. We went there to minister to him, but as we spent the night it was evident that we were the ones being ministered to by Pastor Jim & Irene, even though she was gone. It was a great time in the Lord.

Robert Parmenter – A special friend & support to Irene and Jim and to the Ministry of Project L.A.M.B.S. International Inc. Also can cook a great Newfoundland dinner (JIGS Dinner).

Dear Jim,

Christian greetings in Jesus!

Just a short note to say Gladie and I are remembering you tonight. We are wondering how you are?

Days and nights have to be lonely. Irene was a strong kingpin beside you building your home and ministry. We want you to know we are praying for you. May God grant you His strength and courage for every day and night. Look to Him. Irene is with Jesus, we can't bring her back but it will not be long and we will be with her and Jesus. What consolation, rest in this peace, He has prepared a place!

In His Care,
Arthur Alagore

Home going!

I didn't hear until Thursday of Irene's home going – the 8th was the 3rd anniversary for Cam and Wednesday night we had a memorial honouring him and his legacy to us… the guys decided not to let me know until Thursday.

The note I received was on the corner of my desk. You hadn't said where you'd taken Irene to the hospital so I felt you wanted only family. But I'd decided that Thursday afternoon I was going to call and ask permission to be able to go see her or find out if indeed you were limiting her time to family.

I wish I had something profound to say that would in any way ease the pain but grief doesn't work like that. You walk through it a day at a time. Thank God for the precious Holy Spirit – He only lets in as much reality as we can bear at the time.

You were blessed with a wonderful wife and at times like this, good memories are like oil that flows over and helps heal us.

You and yours are in my prayers.

God strengthen and guide you in the days ahead.

In Christ,
Jacquie Fontaine

≈≈

Hi Jim,

Shirley and I are saddened to hear of the untimely passing of your beloved wife and best friend, Irene. We would like to express our deepest condolences, sincere love and prayerful support to you and your family at this emotionally difficult time.

I know that the fragrance of her beautiful life will forever linger ever so sweetly in your heart as well as in the hearts of those whom she has influenced throughout her earthly sojourning. Irene will be sorely missed, but certainly not forgotten.

Every angel must return to his or her original place of abode and Irene is no different.

May she now retire from all of life's woes and enjoy her quiet repose. *Precious in the sight of the LORD is the death of His saints. (Ps. 116:15)*

Compassionately,
Patrick & Shirley Rimple

≈≈

Dear Jim,

Charlotte and I were very saddened when we heard of Irene's passing. Though we all long for our heavenly home, we are not ready or expecting it now for Irene. We know however that through Jesus she was prepared and we look forward to speaking with her again in heaven some day.

We feel such a loss of words at this time. What few words we have put down seem so inadequate in delivering the comfort we long for them to bring.

May the "God of all comfort" bring the comfort and peace that only He can bring and may they be more tangible today and in the days ahead, than you have ever experienced.

Ernest & Charlotte Goertzen
Assistant Pastor – Springs Church

~~~~~~

Email received: February 1, 2005
Dear Precious People,

I wanted you to know that I love you both and that I am praying for you. I wrote this song yesterday and felt compelled to send it to you. I hope and pray that it will minister to you.

With loving concern,
Tilly

Numbers 6:24-26
The Lord bless you and keep you; the Lord make His face to shine upon you, and be gracious to you; the Lord lift up His countenance upon you, and give you peace.
~~~~~~

2 Thessalonians 2:16-17
Now may our Lord Jesus Christ Himself, and our God and Father, who has loved us and given us everlasting consolation and good hope by grace, comfort your hearts and establish you in every good word and work.
Jude 24-25
Now to Him who is able to keep you from stumbling, and to present you faultless before the presence of His glory with exceeding joy, to God our Saviour, who alone is wise, be glory and majesty, dominion and power, both now and forever. Amen.

IT IS I   Jan 30, 2005

Deep wounds cry out for a deep Saviour
One who is touched with our infirmities
See here, He so gently whispers
Stretch forth your hand
And touch My side,
Feel there the wound, I too have cried
In the darkness of the night
Do not doubt My love, oh child
For it is I.

Chorus:
It is I, It is I
I will not break the reed that's bruised
For it is I.
I see your wounds
I hear your cry
A healing balm I will provide
Pouring in the oil and wine
Be not afraid, my child for it is I

Passing through the vale of weeping
His arms enfold you in the dark night of the soul
He would say with tender compassion

Be not dismayed.
Child do not fear
I your Comforter am near
You will always find Me here
Oh rest in Me, beloved child
For it is I.

Tilly

≈≈

Hi Jim,

On behalf of my wife and myself and my congregation, I would like to extend our deepest sympathies on Irene's passing. Your loss makes us all aware of the brevity of life. We have been praying for you and Irene for some time and we will continue to pray for you and your family.

Again, we grieve with you on your loss. Our love and prayers are with you.

In Christ,
Your brother, **Rick Orsten**

≈≈

Jim,

I just received word of your loss. I'm so sorry! I haven't told Patty or Rachel yet. Rachel will be devastated, as she really connected with both of you, and especially Irene.

You are in my thoughts and prayers!

In Christ,
Paul Vallee

≈≈

Jim, Rachel & Joshua

We cannot express our deep, deep sadness for your loss. Words seem so cheap, but Irene was such a testimony of everything that is good in this world. She will be missed by many, but especially her family. Her spirit will live on in the characters of her children and grandchildren.

Many prayers on your behalf.

Kelly & Karen Friesen

Dear Jim & Family,

Irene will be greatly missed, but we sorrow not as those who have no hope. May God's presence strengthen and sustain you during this time of bereavement.

Our love and prayers are with you.

With love in Jesus,
Roger & Marge Armbruster

Dear Jim,

"Our citizenship is in heaven. And we eagerly await a Saviour from there, the Lord Jesus Christ, who by the power that enables Him to bring everything under His control; will transform our lowly bodies, so that they will be like His glorious body." Philippians 3:20-21.

My memories of Irene are sweet and she was compassionate; always asking us how we are doing. Irene was also a regal saint, giving of herself to others. I will not forget her.

I am praying for you.

Love, **Bertha**

≈≈

To Jim & Family,

Your wife and mother was a saintly woman. Great things will happen for you, the family, because of your Mom's faithful heart and devotion to you. Thank God!

Bertha

≈≈

I remember her saying she wanted to be free as a bird. How free she is, and forever beautiful!

We love you,
The Broesky Family

≈≈

May the mantel of God's love, grace, peace, comfort, power and sustainability be yours in all fullness and completeness. Irene was a very special "lady saint" in our lives. Jim you are very special to us as well.

God bless you. Praying for you.

With all our love,
Allen & Sharon Broesky

~~~~~~

Jim!

Sorry to hear of your loss. Irene will be greatly missed. She has touched many, many lives. She was an inspiration to many, and even in her passing, many lives will be touched.

Our prayers are with you and your family.

Robert & Jackie Parmenter

~~~~~~

Jim!

May you find the peace in Him in whom we believe. Irene is rejoicing. Let us rejoice with her!

God Bless You!
Robert Parmenter

~~~~~~
~~~~~~

Dear Jim, Joshua, Rachel & Families,

It was with deep sadness that we received the news of the reoccurrence of disease in Irene's body. Our hearts of love and our prayers were and are for you in your loss today. We all feel the loss of this wonderful woman of God. Irene was an inspiration of cheer and a refreshing person of consistent faith and true grace. Together with you, we loved and appreciated her deeply.

In light of her severe suffering, we rejoice in the hope of her entrance into the presence of Jesus and her heavenly home. May the wonderful memories you have of Irene, -- together with God's promises of joy provide a great source of comfort and encouragement for your family. Your wife, mother, and grandmother was God's gift to you – and to all who knew her.

On behalf of our church fellowship, we wish to express our heartfelt appreciation for the gift of Irene's ministry to this church and community while you lived and pastored here. In addition, Irene was a blessing to us in your visits to this community in the years since. Her testimony, presence, and work will not be forgotten. May God's grace and peace bring blessing to each of you.

Sincerely in Christ,

Pastor Glen Forsberg
From all of your friends at McMurray Gospel Assembly

Jim,

May God bless you and comfort you. Irene will be receiving her crown of which she is so deserving. She served her Lord, whom she loved as long as she could.

Psalm 121

Songs in the Night

I have been through the valley of weeping,
The valley of sorrow and pain;
But the God of all comfort was with me,
At hand to uphold and sustain.

As the earth needs the cloud and the sunshine,
Our souls need both sorrow and joy;
So He places us oft in the furnace,
The dross from the gold to destroy.

When He leads through some valley of trouble,
His powerful hand we can trace;
For the trials and sorrows He sends us,
Are part of His lessons of grace.

Oft we shrink from the purging and pruning,
Forgetting the Husbandman knows;
The deeper the cutting and paring,
The richer the cluster that grows.

Well He knows that affliction is needed,
He has a wise purpose in view;
And in the dark valley He whispers,
"Hereafter you'll know what I do."

As we travel through life's shadowed valley,
Fresh springs of His love ever rise;
And we learn that our sorrows and losses,
Are blessings just sent in disguise.

So we'll follow wherever He leadeth,
Though pathways be dreary or bright;
For we've proof that our God can give comfort,
Our God can give songs in the night.

Love & Prayers,
Peter & Tina Buhler

≈≈

Dear Jim and Family,

Gentle, gracious, compassionate at this time of great loss and sorrow.

Irene is now seeing Jesus face to face and glorifying Him and rejoicing in His presence!

Love in Christ,
Sylvia & Peter Fehr

≈≈

Jim & Family,

Our Sympathy and Love

"I am always with you;
You hold me by my right hand.
You guide me with Your counsel,
and afterward You will take me into glory----
My flesh and my heart may fail,
but God is the strength of my heart
and my portion forever."

Psalm 73:23, 24 & 26

We treasure the moments and the memories we had and have with you and Irene. The times in Jamaica were extra special.

We love you and are praying for you.

Winston & Viola Penner

≈≈

Dear Jim,

Irene has touched our hearts and lives and will be missed dearly. She has been a mentor, and a vision to me of what being a Godly woman is.

We pray God's abundant blessing on Project L.A.M.B.S. – what started as Irene's and your vision.

All our Love,
Steve & Gloria Wall

≈≈

Dear Brother Jim and family,

"Gathering Home"

Though "earth hath no sorrow
That heaven cannot heal"
We still grieve today
Until that bright tomorrow.

By leaning on His Grace
Our burden can grow lighter
Until we see His face
That makes all heaven brighter.

So carry on your journey
Though Irene has gone ahead,
Knowing you shall meet together
For she ever lives, not dead
Beyond the veil in His Presence
Already rejoicing at His Throne
Anticipating gladness
When the family gathers home.

You are in our hearts and remembered in our prayers.

Love in Christ,
Pastor George Bradley
&Congregation of
Liberty Christian Assembly

Dear Pastor Jim & Family,

Oh, how we will miss our dear, dear Irene – her tender, gentle ways, her soft voice and laughter and her sweet smile!!

It's comforting to know we will see her again in heaven, but we will miss her greatly in the meanwhile.

Please know that you are all in our thoughts and prayers.

We love you,
Peter & Monica Pytel

≈≈

Dear Pastor Jim,

We will cherish all our memories of Pastor Irene. She held a very dear place in our hearts, as do you, so know that we uphold you before God in our prayers, with an ache in our hearts. She has gone on home ahead of us and we rejoice for her. Yet our loss of her presence, even for a short time on this earth, brings us such sorrow. We cannot imagine your own sorrow.

We love you very much Pastor Jim.

All our thoughts & prayers,
Guy & Sheila
Michael & Matthew

≈≈

Dear Jim and family,

YOU ARE BELOVED

You are beloved; you have walked before me with integrity
And I have beheld your heart; I have long gazed at it
To miss you in any way, so know, please know
That I have not gone away, that I will comfort you in this sorrow
That I have not gazed lightly, or in passing, at your heart's pain
I have looked so deeply, so deeply aware of the pain
So deeply aware of your pain
Thank you for letting me lead and guide.
I love you so very deeply, so very deeply
You have not slipped through my fingers
You have never slipped through my fingers
I am resident in your pain; I am resident in your grief
My eyes see with the understanding of a God who knows
I see what others cannot comprehend
I see paths and I see journeys through brambles
It matters not; I walk through any, and every circumstance
You cannot lose me, you cannot lose me
I am the One who sees, the One who knows
And who offers shelter when none is to be found
In the desert places, stormy places, grieving places
I offer a shelter of compassion, a shelter of companionship
In and to your grief, for I am acquainted with all your ways.
I am acquainted with your grief.
I know you do not know this road, but I have promised to never leave or forsake.
Never will I leave or forsake you, for I have surrounded you with my arms.
My arms hold your grief, and hold your soul.
My arms are everlasting, as is my mercy and loving kindness.
I have not removed my arms of help from you.
There is a place where nothing but I can reach.

I will lift you up no matter how low the valley
I have not brought you this far to abandon you.
Not only do I know where you are, right now,
But I care so very deeply about the future.
I care so very deeply about everything that touches your lives
Not once have I forgotten to know you.
I do not forget who you are; I see how deep this pain is.
It feels like you have lost more than you can lose
I plead with you to trust Me, trust my heart
Do not lean on your own understanding, even here I am with you.
I do not take lightly, oh children hear me
I do not take lightly, your hearts pain.
I hear before you cry out, and I hear when there are no words.
I never let go, I never let go.
For I know the plans I have for you saith the Lord.
Plans for a future and a hope, for peace and for comfort
All of these are my provision for you.
It might be hard to see, but there is light.
It will break like the dawn and give you rest,
It will give you rest, there is hope that fadeth not away
You may not see it now, not yet; you feel so much pain.
I have your hand.

All our sympathy and prayers go out to you at this difficult time.
We stand with you in the Lord.

Jeannine & Len Perry

≈≈≈

Pastor Humphries & Family,

Our condolences go out to you. We are indeed saddened by the passing of Sister Irene. We truly admired her work and her thoughtfulness of others. She will always be remembered. We have the pictures she created for us in the album she gave us. Our children recognized her and Andy. We will be praying for you all and God will continue to bless you as you work in His name. We want to thank you for all the assistance and kindness you offered us. You and Sister Irene have been a great help. Junior & I will be here for you when you need someone in Jamaica to reach out to.

We will be praying for you and the family; as God will continue to shine His light on all of you. We'll keep in touch and we will be praying for you.

Love you all,
Sister Carol, Junior & Family
(Jessica & Jeyda)

≈≈

Jim & Family,

We wanted to let you know how much we loved and respected Irene. She was truly (one of) the most amazing women we feel we ever had or will have the privilege of meeting. She was always encouraging and pleasant. She touched a lot of people, including us.

May God comfort you, but be comforted knowing she fulfilled her mission on earth, and is in God's company now!

Love,
Conrad & Kristine

≈≈

Dear Jim,

As we reflected on Irene's life this past week, and then wondered how we could help you; only one thing comes to mind and that is to pray.

I remember when someone close passed away and the one thing that brought me joy was the memories people shared. Jim, the only thing I can think of is the feelings I got being around Irene...JOY! LOVE! PEACE!

Jim, I cannot tell you the eternal impact Irene made on my life and the life of my family. Irene lived a life that was an example.

We come today with such mixed emotions. We are happy for Irene; concern and great love for you. Oh and let's not forget the anticipation of dancing with Irene on streets of gold. In the weeks, months and years to come we are here for you. We will pray for you and we will love you.

All our love and prayers,
Cari, Glenn, Riley, Bradyn, Ally, Sydnie

≈≈

Dear Jim,

Our Heavenly Father has much larger plans than we have. When He takes home a loved one, so precious to us, and a great blessing to others, we are puzzled. One day the veil will be lifted and we will understand. Until then, we know God cares for us.

May God bless and comfort you and yours.

Gordan & Maril Setterlund

≈≈

Dear Jim,

I was so sorry to hear about Irene…and you, Joshua and Rachel are in my thoughts and my prayers….

It's so hard losing the ones we love… They always say everything happens for a reason, and being a Pastor maybe you agree with that but when we lost my sister Luann 10 years ago, it was devastating, we watched her suffer for 3 years, she went from praying and hoping for a miracle to praying for God to take her away from all the pain and suffering… Then 6 years ago we lost Dad and nine months after that we lost Mom, and if you remember way back…we were all very close to Mom and Dad…They say that time heals the pain, I don't believe that, I believe that time just teaches you how to deal with the loss…so it's hard to understand the reasons for losing the ones we love….

I remember how good of a Pastor you were…you really cared about us…and you taught me a lot of things…you taught me about God, and those Thursday night prayer meetings at Aunt Birdies you taught me about the Bible…and then you baptized me in the lake…oh and remember that school bus you had? You taught me how to bleed the brakes on it. Do you remember that? You are the kind of Pastor that is for real...My Mom went to church for many many years and the Pastor would NOT perform her funeral because he was heading off on holidays the day after she died and he wouldn't cancel his trip for one day to perform her service…We had to get a stranger to do it… and at that time I was wishing for you…because I know you wouldn't have treated us like that and Mom always thought highly of you and Irene…I can't believe how that Pastor deserted us when we needed him most…so it kind of makes one wonder about the people who say they are doing God's work…but I never doubted you and your work for God. I don't know why, but I just needed you to know that.

I just wanted to tell you how sorry I am about Irene…and that you are in my thoughts.

Sincerely yours,
Justine Byers (Peany)

Dear Jim & Family,

We were so sorry to hear about Irene. Our thoughts and prayers are with you. We find comfort knowing Irene is with the Lord in glory.

Irene was a very good friend as we were growing up and later God used her and Perrie to bring me to salvation. She was very sweet and we will all miss her.

All our love,
Pastor Dan & Janet Peters

Like the ripples of a stone thrown into a pond, Irene's impact for Christ in the life of others and the love and compassion she showed to all will go on and on --- reaching across this age that is and the age to come --- even as it is still going on in my life.

"Be strong and courageous---do not be discouraged, for the Lord, your God will be with you wherever you go." Joshua 1:9

With much love, your sister in Christ,
Carole Argo

Dear Jim and Family,

Our sincerest condolences are extended to you on the passing of Irene. We will remember her as a vivacious, valiant and victorious sister in God's great family.

May God give you comfort and strength for the days ahead.

Our love and prayers,
Wes & Kay McLeod & Family

Jim,

On behalf of the Community Club and the community, I wish to express our sympathy on the loss of your wife, Irene. Besides a wife, your loss is much deeper I would imagine, because Irene was so much more. I had the honour of meeting Irene twice; once when she spoke at the Marchand Chapel, and a second time at Carol's Bible Study. Jim: Irene deeply impacted my life, seeing how serene and full of life she was; and how the love of God shone on her face; these things about Irene I will never forget, and I know other people will remember her the same way.

God be with you,
Gabi & The Marchand Community Club.

Dear Jim,

Irene was a beautiful woman of God and we've all been enriched by knowing her. Though it means great loss for you and your family, we're also glad that she is finally home with Jesus.

We are praying for you. Looking forward to the great reunion.

Rev. 21:3-4

Love,
Elmer & Carlana Chen

Dear Jim,

I am sending you this poem, which reminds me of Irene. I found it when my mother died and found comfort in it. My Mom loved her roses. She died on the day that Irene died in 1998. When I read this poem now, it will have a double meaning.

"The Rose Beyond the Wall"

Near shady wall a rose once grew,
Budded and blossomed
in God's free light.
Watered and fed by morning dew
Shedding its sweetness day and night.

As it grew and blossomed,
Fair and tall.
Slowly rising to loftier heights
It came to a crevice in the wall,
Through which there shone
A beam of light.

Onward it crept with added strength
With never a thought of fear or pride.
It followed the light
Through the crevice – length
And unfolded itself on the other side.

The light, the dew, the broadening view,
Were found the same as they were before
And it lost itself in beauties new.
Breathing its fragrance more and more.

Shall claim of death cause us to grieve?
And make our courage faint or fall?
Nay, let us faith and hope receive
The rose still grows beyond the wall.

Scattering fragrance far and wide
Just as it did in the day of yore,
Just as it did on the other side
Just as it will forever more.

----A.L. Frink

In memory of Irene Humphries, a friend March 9, 2005.

Keeping you in my prayers.
Bertha Friesen

≈≈

Dear Irene,

You have made a profound impact on my life. You have taught me by your example. Your courage, strength, faith, love and encouragement to all those you had contact with. You have left a legacy.

"Well done good and faithful servant…enter into the joy of your Master." Matthew 25:2

Love, **Karen Friesen**

≈≈

Dear Bro Jim Humphries

Our deepest concern and love go out from Doris and I over the news of Irene passing away. We have been so very busy the last month or more as we have moved to Cranbrook, B.C. What we have to do now is to remember the tremendous times we had together in Jamaica. That is and was a wonderful time with you and Irene. We will always remember the sweet times we spent and the joy that you and Irene brought to the Jamaican Saints.

This is a new move for Doris and me in moving to Cranbrook. We have to do some building on to our place here. Right now we are trying to catch up on the big move here. Doris and I both felt the Lord leading us here. We don't know what God has for us here. God knows and we feel good in the Lord's leading.

Loving prayers,
From Doris & Borge

Prayer

The Lord always hears our prayer,

But He does not always say, 'Yes!'
Sometimes He says, 'Wait,'
Sometimes He says, 'No;'
For He has something better for us.

God's delays are not denials,
He has heard your prayer;
He knows all about your trials,
Knows you every care.

God's delays are not denials,
Help is on the way;
He is watching o'er life's dials,
Bringing forth that day.

God's delays are not denials,
You will find Him true;
Working through the darkest trials,
What is best for you.

Hope this poem will be a blessing to you.

Love,
Liesa & Pete

Dear Pastor Jim,

Although the funeral and its' preparations may now seem only but a blur in time, I'm sure the void in your life of having lost Sister Irene is still often too clear and perhaps overwhelming. Most of us during times like these, would that we could say or do something to somehow ease the pain for the one left behind. You, yourself, have your own cross to bear in this matter and have had numerous times over the years prior to her departure. Yet, no one can really know your pain, nor your feelings of despair or loneliness. These, are deeply personal and intricately woven into a lifetime of memories, sharing dreams, goals, family, common interests, discussion, prayer and intimacy. She wasn't you, nor you her, but together you were the fabric that many fondly referred to as the Humphries'.

As much as I or we, your Church Family are lost for words, we are comforted in this, that you know well "Our Deeply Personal Loving Heavenly Father". He knows with perfect timeliness, the right things to say and do, each and every moment.

Sending Christian love and prayers!
Pastor Barry Hurren
& Your Dayspring Family

≈≈

Dear Pastor Humphries,

Let me, on behalf of all members in all our churches, greet you in the name of our Blessed Lord and wish for you the joy of the Lord.

It is now clear to us that your coming to Jamaica and specifically to our Independent Assemblies was a type of response to a Macedonian Call as a missionary. This brings joy to our hearts and spiritual upliftment to us all, but especially to all who received training at the Bible Institute which you have developed.

Conversely, we are now saddened by the news of the death of your dear wife and our sister Irene. Our joys became sorrow as we mourn her loss with you.

Our sympathy for you is deep and our sorrow is great, yet we sorrow with a hope that one day, maybe soon, we will meet again.

We know you are a man of faith and hope; hence we will only encourage you to be of good cheer. God understands and although He does not have to explain His reason for whatever He does, He will reveal His will and His reason to you some day. Then, all your sorrows will turn into joy and your tears into laughter.

Pastor Humphries, in God's hands we place you at this time as we pray for you. May His blessings be always upon you.

Fraternally yours,
Bishop N. Hamilton
Independent Assemblies of God of Jamaica

Daily Devotional Tribute

Look from the top
Song of Solomon 4:8

Crushing weights give the Christian wings. It seems like a contradiction in terms, but it is a blessed truth. David out of some bitter experience cried: "*Oh that I had wings like a dove! For then would I fly away, and be at rest*". (Psalm 55:6). But before he finished this meditation he seems to have realized that his wish for wings was a realizable one. For he says, "*Cast thy burden upon the Lord, and He shall sustain thee.*"

The word "burden" is translated in the Bible margin, "what He (Jehovah) hath given thee." The saints' burdens are God-given; they lead him to "wait upon Jehovah," and when that is done, in the magic of trust, the "burden" is metamorphosed into a pair of wings, and the weighted one "mounts up with wings as eagles."

From Sunday School Times
Streams in the Desert
Mrs. Charles E. Couman

SONG OF PRAISE TRIBUTE

For Those Tears I Died

You said you'd come and share all my sorrows
You said you'd be there for all my tomorrows
I came so close to sending you away
And just like you promised, you came there to stay
I just had to pray.

And Jesus said, "Come to the water stand by my side,
I know you are thirsty, you won't be denied.
I felt every teardrop when in darkness you cried,
And I strove to remind you that for those tears I died."

Your goodness so great I can't understand,
And, dear Lord, I know that all this was planned.
Saviour, you're here now, and always will be.
Your love is so great and always so free,
Jesus and me.

Jesus, I give you my heart and my soul,
I know, without you I'd never be whole.
Saviour, you opened up all the right doors,
And I thank you and praise you from earth's humble shores.
Take me I'm yours.

** *This song was sung on our wedding during the ceremony and was sang again on Irene's home going day*

ROSE OF SHARON

Song of Solomon 2:1-4

I am the rose of Sharon,
the lily of the valleys.

Like a lily among the thorns, so is
my darling among the maidens.

Like an apple tree among the trees
of the forest, so is my beloved
among the young men.

In His shade I took great delight
and sat down, And his fruit was
sweet to my taste.

He has brought me to His
banquet hall,
And His banner over me is love.

May 2004

A ROSE IN HIS HANDS

≈≈≈≈≈≈≈≈≈≈≈≈≈≈≈≈≈≈≈≈

In the beginning of April 2004, I received a card from a precious sister in the Lord. It was very special because she had made it herself. On the front was a magazine picture of a rose being cradled in someone's hands with the words, **"The most precious and delicate rose is held in the Father's hands."** *Inside she wrote...*

Dear Sister Irene,
I don't dare question or ask why; I just watch you and learn that by this time, you are on a higher ground. I was told that at the mountaintop are the rarest and most beautiful flowers. Watching you was my most memorable sermon and Godly teaching. Holding you in high esteem before God in my prayer.

A VISION OF A ROSE

≈≈≈≈≈≈≈≈≈≈≈≈≈≈≈≈≈≈

On April 15th 2004, a couple came over to visit and have fellowship with us. As we prayed the young wife rather reluctantly shared a vision she was given while we were praying.

"In my vision, I saw a beautiful rose
and its outer shell was blackened and burnt—I thought it was dead at first, but as I looked on, its outer shell fell off and the inside petals were fresh and beautiful. From the centre of the rose came forth more petals. I asked the Lord what had blackened it so, and He said, "Fire" (trials). I watched as the fire came and the rose again was burnt and the whole process of its outside falling away was repeated. Each time the fire came and the outside fell away,

the rose would produce more petals from its centre. The result was that the rose became larger and larger. I asked what the petals were symbolic of and the answer came that they were converts—people coming to Christ through what you are suffering. The verse also came to mind that which the enemy intends for your harm, ruin and destruction—God will work it out for good as you put your trust in Him."

She and her husband returned the next evening with a rose of an unusual colour. She apologized that this rose was awfully small in comparison to the one in the vision; nevertheless very beautiful.

A RECORD

≈≈≈≈≈≈≈≈≈≈

I write these things to record the special way in which God is speaking to me in the midst of the fiery furnace.

When I first learned that the ovarian cancer was back in March 2004, my first response was like that of Daniel's friends, Shadrach, Meshach, and Abed-Nego, who believed the God they served was able to deliver them from the burning fiery furnace and from the evil intent of king Nebuchadnezzar. But if the Lord did otherwise, they would still worship the God of Israel above all (Daniel 3).

I know that once again, I am in the fiery furnace; yet in my heart I know that God is able to deliver me in the midst of this trial and from the devastation of this disease. If He does not I will continue to worship Him, and declare that He is the One I love and serve alone.
He is wonderful!

I am the rose of Sharon, and the lily of the valleys.
Song of Solomon 2:1

Please continue to remember us in your prayers.

Irene Humphries
Box 20569 Steinbach, MB R5G 1R9

THANKS

I want to say a special thanks to all of you who spoke so many words of encouragement into Irene's life. It just shows forth to a lost world that there is true strength and hope in the body of Christ. Those things that you have said and done are now locked into the time line of all eternity. You were all part of the journey that moulded and made Irene into who she was and is. God used you to create a treasure that has honoured Him.

The journey of creation and building of character to the last days of transformation have all been guided and carefully worked by God's Holy Spirit. He worked through you and in her life as well. The potter has moulded and formed a vessel of Irene that has brought much honour to His name.

Thank you all for being willing to be a tool in God's hands for His Glory. We are grateful beyond words. You have helped take a lump of clay and with the help of Christ build a lasting treasure for His glory.

APPENDIX

Liquid Sunshine

Irene's personal relationship with Christ:

When Irene was twelve years old she was walking home from a church that she attended in Union, Ontario and her thoughts where on the verse that she heard the teacher share in Sunday School earlier that morning. It was John 3:16,

> "For God so loved the world that He gave His only begotten Son, that whosoever believes in Him shall not perish, but have eternal life."

She prayed that Christ would come into her heart and immediately she said she felt like she was completely covered all over with liquid sunshine. She had become part of the family of Christ and her life would never be the same again. God had opened the door into her heart and placed a beautiful treasure of His great love in there.

If Irene's life has spoken to you and you want that heavenly treasure as your own. Just take a moment to pray this prayer like so many others have and you to will become part of the body and family of Jesus Christ.

Relationship Prayer:

Dear Jesus,

I confess that I am a sinner, having gone my own way and that I need you as my Lord and Saviour. I believe that You paid the price for my sins when You died on the cross and shed Your blood for me, so that I might have eternal life. I am ready and willing to turn from my sin and return to You. I now invite You into my heart and surrender the control and direction of my life entirely to You. Help me to be a true disciple to You and to others. Thank you for taking my punishment and providing for me a way of escape from eternal death to an everlasting life. Thank you for coming into my heart so that I can now have a close personal relationship with You. Amen.

My Relationship Commitment:

My Confession:

I have confessed my sinfulness to God, turned from my sin and believe that Christ has forgiven me.

My Acceptance:

I now receive the living Christ into my heart as Saviour.

My Commitment:

I surrender the right of my life to Jesus Christ. Jesus is my Lord.

Date of surrender to Christ:

____

Signature:

____

Witnessed by:

____

My Relationship Home:

Welcome into the personal family of Christ. Today is the first day of the rest of your life. You are now part of a world-wide family.

You no longer need to be empty or alone, no matter the circumstances or the trials that you may find yourself in. You now have a companion that sticks closer than a brother. He is with you 24 hours a day. All you have to do is call upon His name and share your heart openly with Him.

Remember He will never leave you nor forsake you. If you stumble or fall, just ask Jesus Christ to help you up again.

Discipleship is relationship and relationship is a walk of discipleship in Jesus Christ. The two must go hand-in-hand if we are to have that personal, intimate relationship with our Lord Jesus Christ.

My Relationship Testimony:

Now that you have made this decision for Christ you should try to share it with somebody like a family member or friend or even with me. I would love to hear from you and help you with your new life in Christ.

Dr. James P. Humphries
Box 20569 Steinbach Manitoba R5G 1R9

Or Email me at projectlambs@mts.net

APPENDIX

Obituary

IRENE BEATRICE HUMPHRIES 1950 - 2005

After a lengthy illness our loving wife, mother and grandmother passed on to be with the Lord Jesus Christ on Wednesday March 9, 2005 at St. Boniface Hospital in Winnipeg, Manitoba, with her loving family and friends by her side.

Irene was born in St. Thomas, Ontario on March 20th, 1950 to John and Gerda Heights. She was the middle child of three, an older sister Dorothy and younger brother Gary who live in St. Thomas. At the age of twelve, after hearing John 3:16 in Sunday School she invited Christ to come into her heart as Lord and Saviour while walking home from church. She said it was receiving "liquid sunshine all over her." Irene graduated from Arthur Voaden Secondary School in 1970 where she lived in Union Ontario.

She then went on to complete a Registered Nursing Assistant program course at Simcoe Ontario. After graduation she worked in the Toronto area for a short period of time. From there she worked for Jesus to the Communist World which today is called Voice of the Martyrs. She was also involved as a summer missionary for Child Evangelism.

Even as a young teenager she felt a call to missions, but it was not until the latter years of her life when she began to fulfill that dream to travel and teach as a missionary.

During the "Jesus People Movement" while Irene was working as a volunteer in a coffee house ministry she met a street evangelist named Jimmer (James Humphries). They were married six weeks later on July 8, 1972. This was an exciting time because Irene's home church was experiencing revival under the ministry of the Setara twins. During almost

33 years of marriage God blessed them with a son Joshua and daughter-in-law Donna and a daughter Rachel and son-in-law Kobbie. As well, they were blessed with five grandchildren – Adrianna, Jeremy, Sadie, Tyah and Anna-Irene, as well as son-in-law James.

Over the years Irene has served in a variety of ministries. The first was developing and producing a children's TV program called the Happiness Club. From there she was involved in a church plant in Port Stanley, Ontario. Over the years, she has worked in a variety of ministries across Canada. With her husband, they have pastored in Fingal, Ontario, Ernfold, Saskatchewan, Fort McMurray, Alberta and three different opportunities in Steinbach, Manitoba. In 1996, she became co-founder and co-director of Project L.A.M.B.S. International. This lead to writing and teaching in a variety of countries. She has traveled to Jamaica, Mexico, Ukraine, Germany, Myanmar, Israel and throughout Canada and the USA.

In April of 2000, she was ordained by the Independent Assemblies of God in Jamaica, in Canada under the Fellowship of Christian Ministries by Pastor Peter Broesky and the Fellowship of Christian Assemblies by Dayspring Fellowship in Ste. Anne.

Irene was an accomplished artist, poet and writer – receiving various awards throughout her life.

Over the same period of time Irene completed a course at Winnipeg South Technical School in production art and a business course at the Federal Business Development Bank. Irene has also taken courses from Ontario Bible College, Prairie Bible Institute and Briercrest Bible College. In 2001, Irene graduated with her MA degree in Global Christian Studies with a minor in TESL from Providence Theological Seminary.

In the fall of 2002, Irene had emergency surgery which showed that she had an extensive case of ovarian cancer. She was greatly helped by the new Palliative Care Program in Manitoba. For a period of time God gave her extra days to continue to minister and travel twice to Jamaica as well as Myanmar. Cancer came back again in October 2004 with much pain and challenges. The last number of months were very stressful for Irene because the cancer pain was very hard to control.

She leaves to mourn her beloved husband Jim, son Joshua and daughter-in-law Donna, daugher Rachel and son-in-law Kobbie, grandchildren Adrienna, Jeremy, Sadie, Tyah and Anna-Irene and son-in-law James. She was predeceased by her father John Haight in 1996 and by her mother Gerda Haight in 1997.

Irene and James and the family wish to extend special thanks to all the many friends who helped us walk this challenging journey. To her care coach Matilda Fehr, as well as Dr. Krahn and Anne Plett, for all the long hours of ministry and help. To the Cancer Care staff of nurses and doctors we say thank you. Also, a special thanks to all the doctors and staff at St. Boniface Hospital in Winnipeg who with much care, love and gentleness, ministered and served Irene with great affection in those last two and a half weeks. We as a family are greatly indebted to you all.

The viewing will be held at Irene's home church (Gospel Chapel) in LaBroquerie on Monday, March 13 at 7:00pm. The funeral will take place at the Steinbach Mennonite Church on Tuesday, March 15 at 10:00am. Internment to follow at Heritage Cemetery. Arrangements entrusted to Birchwood Funeral Chapel, Steinbach, Manitoba.

In memory of Irene, donations can be made to Project LAMBS "Memorial Fund" to commemorate the memory of Irene and her service for the Lord Jesus Christ as a teacher and servant. It was her desire that this fund be used to help train women for full time ministry. These checks may be sent to Project LAMBS, Box 20569, Steinbach, MB, R5G 1R9.